The Ultimate Air Fryer Cookbook for Beginners

1700 Days Mouthwatering and Effortless Air Fryer Recipes for Beginners with Tips & Tricks to Fry, Grill, and Bake

Mario D. Payne

Contents

Introduction 1
What Are Air Fryers? 1
How to Choose an Air Fryer? 2
What Can You Cook in an Air Fryer and What
Foods to Avoid? 3
The Benefits of Air Fryers 4
Cleaning and Maintaining Your Air Fryer ... 5
Care Tips for Your Air Fryer 6
Frequently Asked Questions 7

Chapter 1: Breakfast Recipes 8
Crispy Hash Brown Birds' Nests 8
Savory Stuffed Bell Pepper Omelette Bombs 8
Maple Glazed Bacon Cinnamon Rolls 8
Cheesy Spinach and Artichoke Frittata Muffins
.... 9
Pesto and Sun-Dried Tomato Egg Bites 9
Sweet Potato and Black Bean Breakfast Tacos 9
Blueberry-Lemon Ricotta Pancake Poppers 10
Zucchini and Goat Cheese Egg White Wraps 10
Caramelized Onion and Mushroom Breakfast
Quesadillas 10
Chicken and Waffle Sliders with Sriracha
Honey Butter 11
Spinach and Feta Stuffed French Toast Roll-
Ups 11
Crispy Prosciutto and Brie Breakfast Pizza 12
Apple Cinnamon Quinoa Breakfast Bowls... 12
Lemon Poppy Seed Pancake Bites with
Blueberry Compote............................ 13
Peanut Butter and Jelly Stuffed French Toast
Bites 13
Blackberry Cobbler 13
Strawberry Banana Bread 14
Cheesy Air Fryer Garlic Bread 14
Mozzarella Sticks with Marinara Sauce 14
Full English Breakfast........................ 15
Pumpkin Pudding with Vanilla Wafers 15
Crispy Bacon and Egg Pie Recipe 16
Devilled Kidneys Recipe 16

Shropshire Fidget Pie 16

Chapter 2: Main Recipes 17
Cajun Stuffed Bell Peppers 17
Chimichurri Marinated Steak with Roasted
Vegetables 17
Garlic Parmesan Pork Chops with Roasted
Brussels Sprouts 18
Teriyaki Glazed Salmon with Sesame Broccoli
.... 18
Crispy Buttermilk Fried Chicken with Honey
Mustard Sauce................................... 19
Mediterranean Stuffed Eggplant Boats 19
Thai Red Curry Coconut Chicken with Jasmine
Rice 20
Buffalo Cauliflower "Wings" with Ranch
Dipping Sauce................................... 20
Moroccan Spiced Lamb Meatballs with Yoghurt
Sauce 21
Pesto and Mozzarella Stuffed Chicken Breast
with Roasted Asparagus 21
Balsamic Glazed Pork Tenderloin with Roasted
Vegetables 22
Sesame Ginger Tofu with Stir-Fried Vegetables
.... 23
Mexican-Style Stuffed Bell Peppers with Black
Beans and Corn 23
Lemon Herb Roasted Cornish Hens with
Herbed Quinoa 24
Sweet and Spicy Honey Sriracha Glazed
Salmon with Roasted Sweet Potatoes......... 24
Korean Bulgogi Beef Lettuce Wraps with
Pickled Vegetables 25
Mediterranean Grilled Vegetable Skewers with
Lemon-Herb Couscous 26
Honey Mustard Glazed Turkey Breast with
Hasselback Potatoes 26
Cajun Shrimp and Sausage Foil Packets with
Corn on the Cob 27
Spicy Chipotle Lime Chicken Fajitas with

Charred Peppers and Onions 28
Air Fryer Stuffed Chicken Breast with Spinach and Feta 28
Mexican-Style Stuffed Chicken Breasts ...29

Chapter 3: Fish and Seafood 30
Coconut Curry Cod with Mango Salsa 30
Lemon Dill Salmon Cakes with Caper Remoulade 30
Spicy Tandoori Grilled Fish Tacos with Mint Chutney 31
Teriyaki Glazed Mahi-Mahi with Pineapple Salsa 32
Mediterranean Herb Crusted Sea Bass with Roasted Tomatoes 32
Blackened Scallops with Avocado Lime Crema 33
Harissa Spiced Grilled Shrimp Skewers with Tzatziki Sauce 33
Pesto Parmesan Crusted Halibut with Roasted Vegetables 34
Thai Red Curry Mussels with Coconut Rice 35
Chimichurri Grilled Swordfish with Grilled Corn Salad 35
Baja Fish Tacos with Chipotle Lime Crema and Pickled Onions 36
Szechuan Style Spicy Garlic Shrimp with Stir-Fried Vegetables 37
Mediterranean Stuffed Squid with Lemon and Feta 37
Garlic Butter Grilled Clams with Fresh Herbs 38
Pecan Crusted Red Snapper with Maple Dijon Glaze 38
Sesame Crusted Tuna Steaks with Wasabi Mayo 39
Spicy Mango Glazed Salmon with Quinoa Pilaf 39
Grilled Octopus Salad with Citrus Vinaigrette 40
Air Fryer Baja Fish Tacos 41
Air Fryer Bang Bang Shrimp with Sweet Chilli Sauce 41

Chapter 4: Poultry & Meat Recipes ... 42
Maple Bacon Wrapped Chicken Thighs with Maple Dijon Glaze 42
Jerk Spiced Turkey Burgers with Mango Salsa 42
Thai Basil Chicken Lettuce Wraps with Peanut Sauce 43
Honey Mustard Glazed Pork Belly Bites with Apple Slaw 43
Teriyaki Pineapple Chicken Skewers with Coconut Rice 44
Chipotle Lime Grilled Chicken Tacos with Avocado Crema 44
Balsamic Fig Glazed Duck Breast with Roasted Root Vegetables 45
Cajun Buttermilk Fried Quail with Smoky Remoulade 46
Ginger Soy Glazed Beef Skewers with Sesame Broccoli 46
Vietnamese Lemongrass Grilled Pork with Rice Vermicelli Salad 47
Garlic Parmesan Turkey Meatballs with Marinara Sauce 47
Sriracha Honey Glazed Duck Wings with Pickled Vegetables 48
Panko Crusted Pork Schnitzel with Lemon-Caper Butter Sauce 49
Spicy Jamaican Jerk Chicken Sliders with Pineapple Slaw 49
Moroccan Spiced Grilled Lamb Kebabs with Mint Yoghurt Sauce 50
Szechuan Peppercorn Crusted Beef Stir-Fry with Vegetables 50
Honey Sriracha Glazed Bacon Wrapped Turkey Breast with Roasted Vegetables 51
18 Mango Habanero Glazed Pork Tenderloin with Grilled Pineapple Salsa 52
Pineapple Chicken Skewers 52

Chapter 5: Healthy Vegetables & Fruit 53
Cinnamon Roasted Butternut Squash Wedges with Greek Yoghurt Dip 53
Coconut Lime Brussels Sprouts with Toasted Coconut Flakes 53
Balsamic Glazed Portobello Mushroom Caps

with Goat Cheese 53

Maple Sriracha Roasted Carrot Fries with Greek Yogurt Ranch 54

Spiralized Sweet Potato Noodles with Garlic Parmesan Sauce 54

Sesame Ginger Green Beans with Toasted Almonds 55

Crispy Parmesan Roasted Broccoli Bites ... 55

Mango Habanero Glazed Pineapple Skewers 56

Garlic Rosemary Roasted Root Vegetable Medley 56

Turmeric Infused Roasted Eggplant Rounds with Mint Yogurt Sauce 56

Strawberry Balsamic Bruschetta with Basil and Toasted Baguette Slices 57

Smoky Paprika Roasted Bell Pepper Strips with Cilantro Lime Sauce 57

Grilled Watermelon Skewers with Feta and Mint... 58

Asian Sesame Cucumber Noodle Salad with Peanut Dressing 58

Lemon Dill Roasted Radishes with Greek Yoghurt Dip..................................... 58

Roasted Beet and Goat Cheese Salad with Honey Lime Vinaigrette 59

Spiced Apple Rings with Almond Butter Drizzle... 59

Roasted Portobello Mushroom Cap "Burger" with Avocado and Tomato 60

Honey Lime Glazed Grilled Pineapple Rings with Coconut Whipped Cream 60

Roasted Asparagus Spears with Lemon Garlic Aioli 61

Roasted Brussels Sprouts 61

Zucchini Fritters 61

Cinnamon Apple Chips 62

Parmesan Zucchini Fries...................... 62

Honey-Glazed Carrots 62

Garlic-Parmesan Broccoli 62

Cinnamon-Roasted Butternut Squash........ 63

Stuffed Bell Peppers 63

Buffalo Cauliflower Wings 63

Mediterranean Stuffed Eggplant 64

Air Fryer Hummus-Stuffed Mushrooms...... 64

Garlic Parmesan Roasted Broccoli 64

Chapter 6: Family Favourites (Fast and Easy Everyday) 65

Crunchy Chicken Parmesan Nuggets with Marinara Dipping Sauce 65

Cheesy Beef and Veggie Stuffed Bell Peppers 65

Tex-Mex Loaded Sweet Potato Skins with Guacamole 66

Hawaiian BBQ Chicken Sliders with Pineapple Salsa 66

Crispy Ranch Seasoned Fish Tacos with Lime Crema 67

Teriyaki Glazed Meatball Skewers with Vegetable Fried Rice 67

Spinach and Ricotta Stuffed Shells with Marinara Sauce 68

BBQ Pulled Pork Loaded Nachos with Avocado Lime Crema 69

Caprese Stuffed Chicken Breast with Balsamic Glaze 69

Mexican Street Corn Chicken Quesadillas with Lime Crema 70

Philly Cheesesteak Stuffed Peppers with Provolone Cheese 70

Pesto Turkey Meatball Subs with Mozzarella Cheese... 71

Crispy Taco-Stuffed Zucchini Boats with Salsa 71

Italian Sausage and Pepper Hoagies with Spicy Mustard 72

BBQ Chicken Flatbread Pizzas with Caramelized Onions 72

Teriyaki Glazed Salmon Burgers with Asian Slaw.. 72

BBQ Bacon-Wrapped Stuffed Jalapenos with Cream Cheese 73

Chicken Alfredo Stuffed Shells with Garlic Bread 73

Black Bean Burgers with Chipotle Mayo ... 74

Air Fryer Garlic Knots 74

Air Fryer Cornbread Muffins 75

Cinnamon Sugar Air Fryer Donut Holes ... 75

Chapter 7: Beans & Grains Recipes ...   76

Southwest Quinoa Stuffed Bell Peppers 76

Spicy Cajun Chickpea Fritters with Creole Aioli 76

Moroccan Spiced Lentil Burgers with Mint Yogurt Sauce 77

Black Bean and Quinoa Veggie Burgers with Avocado Lime Aioli 77

Crispy Turmeric Rice Balls with Curry Dipping Sauce 78

Cajun Red Beans and Rice Croquettes with Remoulade Sauce 78

Greek-Style Baked Lima Beans with Feta and Olives 79

Crispy Panko Crusted Wild Rice Cakes with Sriracha Mayo 79

Spicy Chipotle Black Bean Tacos with Lime Slaw 80

Garlic Herb Farro Risotto with Roasted Vegetables 80

Cajun Spiced Black Eyed Pea Fritters with Spicy Remoulade 81

Cheesy Broccoli and Rice Patties with Roasted Red Pepper Sauce 82

Spiced Chickpea and Bulgur Wheat Pilaf with Yogurt Sauce 82

Crispy Quinoa and Vegetable Spring Rolls with Peanut Dipping Sauce 83

Crispy Pinto Bean and Brown Rice Cakes with Cilantro Lime Sauce 83

Spicy Black Bean Tacos with Avocado Crema 84

Air Fryer Falafel with Tahini Sauce 84

Crispy Air Fryer Lentil Fritters 85

Air Fryer Refried Beans 85

Cajun Seasoned Air Fryer Pinto Beans 86

Garlic Parmesan Edamame.................... 86

BBQ Baked Beans with a Crunchy Topping 86

Air Fryer Mexican Street Corn with Black Bean Salsa 87

Crispy Air Fryer Falafel Sliders 87

Air Fryer Three Bean Salad 88

Smoky Air Fryer Red Lentil Dip 88

Spicy Cajun Roasted Chickpeas 88

Buffalo Ranch Roasted Chickpeas 89

Stuffed Air Fryer Bell Peppers with Rice ... 89

Chapter 8: Appetisers and Sides   90

Zucchini Ribbon Fritters with Spicy Marinara Sauce 90

Crispy Bacon-Wrapped Asparagus Bundles with Balsamic Glaze 90

Panko Crusted Avocado Fries with Chipotle Lime Ranch................................ 90

Cheesy Spinach and Artichoke Stuffed Mushrooms 91

Jalapeno Popper Stuffed Mini Bell Peppers   91

Honey Sriracha Glazed Meatballs with Sesame Seeds 92

Spicy Cajun Shrimp Skewers with Remoulade Sauce 92

Crispy Coconut Onion Rings with Pineapple Dipping Sauce............................... 93

Loaded Mexican Street Corn Dip with Tortilla Chips 93

Spicy Tandoori Chicken Skewers with Mint Chutney 94

Greek Spanakopita Triangles with Tzatziki Sauce 94

Smoky Bacon-Wrapped Jalapeno Poppers with Cream Cheese 95

Pesto and Sun-Dried Tomato Pinwheels with Balsamic Glaze 95

Teriyaki Glazed Chicken Meatball Skewers with Peanut Sauce 96

Baked Feta with Honey and Thyme with Toasted Baguette Slices 96

Buffalo Cauliflower and Chickpea Lettuce Wraps with Ranch Dressing 97

Crispy Baked Coconut Shrimp with Mango Salsa 97

Crispy Air Fryer Tofu Bites 98

Crispy Air Fryer Tortilla Chips 98

Cheesy Bacon-Wrapped Jalapeno Poppers with Cream Cheese Filling 98

Introduction

Welcome to the Air Fryer Cookbook For Beginners! I'm thrilled to be sharing my passion for cooking and the amazing possibilities that can be achieved with this versatile kitchen appliance. In these pages, you'll find a collection of delicious and easy-to-follow recipes that will help you make the most out of your air fryer.

Cooking has always been a personal and intimate experience for me. It's a way to express creativity, nurture loved ones, and explore new flavours. I believe that everyone, regardless of their culinary background, can enjoy the pleasure of preparing delicious meals that bring joy and satisfaction to both the cook and the diners.

As a home cook myself, I understand the challenges and hesitations that can arise when trying out new recipes or using a new cooking appliance. That's why this cookbook is designed specifically for beginners. Whether you're a seasoned chef looking to explore the world of air frying or a novice cook stepping into the kitchen for the first time, this book is here to guide you every step of the way.

I want to assure you that you're not alone in this culinary adventure. Throughout this cookbook, I'll be your companion, sharing my knowledge, tips, and personal experiences to help you navigate the world of air frying with confidence and ease. I want you to feel empowered and excited to try new recipes, experiment with flavours, and create delicious meals for yourself, your family, and your friends.

In these pages, you'll find a variety of recipes that showcase the versatility of the air fryer. From crispy appetisers to mouthwatering mains, and even indulgent desserts, there's something for everyone to enjoy. You'll be amazed at how the air fryer can transform your favourite dishes into healthier versions without sacrificing flavour or texture.

So, whether you're looking to whip up a quick weeknight dinner, host a gathering with friends, or simply satisfy your cravings, this cookbook is your go-to guide for unlocking the full potential of your air fryer. Get ready to embark on a culinary journey filled with tantalising aromas, delightful flavours, and the joy of creating memorable meals.

Remember, cooking is a delightful adventure that encourages exploration, creativity, and above all, enjoyment. I encourage you to embrace this journey, make it your own, and have fun along the way. Let's get started and discover the incredible possibilities that await you in the world of air frying!

What Are Air Fryers?

Have you ever wished you could indulge in your favourite crispy, fried foods without the guilt or the hassle of deep frying? Well, say hello to the revolutionary kitchen appliance that's taking the culinary world by storm: the air fryer! If you're wondering what exactly an air fryer is and how it works its magic, you're in the right place. Let's dive in and explore the wonderful world of air fryers.

At first glance, an air fryer might resemble a compact countertop oven, but it's so much more than that. It's a game-changer for anyone looking to enjoy delicious, crispy food with less oil and a fraction of the mess. By using hot air circulation combined with a minimal amount of oil, air fryers create that desirable crispy exterior while locking in moisture, resulting in perfectly cooked dishes.

So, how does it work? Inside the air fryer, there's a powerful heating element and a high-speed fan. When you set the desired temperature and time, the heating element rapidly heats the air inside the fryer while the fan circulates the hot air around the food. This circulating air creates a convection effect, mimicking the process of deep frying but with significantly less oil.

One of the great advantages of air fryers is their ability to cook food evenly and quickly. The hot air penetrates every nook and cranny of the ingredients, ensuring that they cook through evenly and achieve that desired golden brown finish. This means you can enjoy crispy French fries, crunchy chicken wings, or even flaky pastries without the need for excessive oil or lengthy frying times.

But air fryers aren't just limited to frying. They can also be used for baking, roasting, grilling, and even reheating leftovers. From perfectly roasted vegetables to juicy grilled meats, the possibilities are endless. Air fryers are incredibly versatile and can handle a wide variety of dishes, making them a valuable addition to any kitchen.

Aside from the convenience and versatility, one of the major draws of air fryers is their health benefits. By using little to no oil, air fryers significantly reduce the calorie and fat content of your favourite fried foods. This means you can enjoy guilt-free versions of your beloved crispy treats without compromising on taste and texture.

In addition to being healthier, air fryers also offer a cleaner and more hassle-free cooking experience. Say goodbye to the greasy splatters and lingering frying smells that come with traditional deep frying. Air fryers are designed to contain the mess and keep your kitchen clean. Many models also come with dishwasher-safe parts, making cleanup a breeze.

Whether you're a health-conscious individual, a busy parent, or a culinary enthusiast looking to experiment with new cooking techniques, an air fryer is a fantastic addition to your kitchen arsenal. It's a tool that brings convenience, flavour and healthier alternatives to your favourite dishes.

Overall, air fryers are innovative appliances that use hot air circulation and minimal oil to achieve crispy, flavorful results. They offer a healthier alternative to deep frying and provide versatility in cooking a wide range of dishes. With an air fryer, you can enjoy your favourite fried foods guilt-free, with less mess and hassle. So, get ready to elevate your cooking game and savour the delights of crispy perfection with the magic of air frying!

How to Choose an Air Fryer?

Choosing the perfect air fryer for your kitchen can seem like a daunting task with the plethora of options available on the market. But fear not! We're here to guide you through the process and help you find the air fryer that suits your needs and culinary aspirations. So, let's dive in and discover the key factors to consider when selecting your ideal air fryer.

- **Capacity:** The first thing to consider is the capacity of the air fryer. Think about the size of your household and how much food you typically cook. Air fryers come in various sizes, ranging from compact models with a capacity of around 2 litres to larger ones that can hold up to 6 litres or more. If you have a big family or often entertain guests, a larger capacity might be more suitable for you. However, if you have limited kitchen space or cook for one or two people, a smaller capacity might suffice.

- **Power and Cooking Performance**: The power of an air fryer is measured in watts, and it directly affects the cooking performance. Higher wattage means faster cooking times and more efficient heat circulation. Look for models with at least 1500 watts for optimal results. This ensures that your food will cook evenly and achieve that desired crispiness in a shorter amount of time.

- **Temperature Range and Controls**: Check the temperature range offered by the air fryer. Most models have a temperature range of 180°C to 200°C, which is suitable for a wide variety of recipes. However, if you enjoy experimenting with different cooking techniques, look for models that offer a wider temperature range. Additionally, consider the ease of use and controls. Some air fryers come with digital displays and pre-set cooking programs, making it simple to select the desired temperature and cooking time.

- **Additional Features:** Air fryers often come with a range of additional features that can enhance your cooking experience. Some models have built-in timers, adjustable cooking racks, or even multiple cooking functions like baking and grilling. Consider which features are important to you and align with your cooking preferences. For example, if you enjoy baking, look for an air fryer that offers baking capabilities.
- **Ease of Cleaning:** Nobody wants to spend hours scrubbing and cleaning after a delicious meal. Therefore, consider the ease of cleaning when choosing an air fryer. Look for models with non-stick cooking surfaces, removable and dishwasher-safe parts, and accessible nooks and crannies that are easy to wipe clean. This will save you time and effort in maintaining your air fryer.
- **Brand and Reviews:** Lastly, it's always a good idea to do some research on the brand and read customer reviews. Look for reputable brands that have a track record of producing quality appliances. Customer reviews can provide valuable insights into the performance, durability, and overall satisfaction of the air fryer you're considering.

By considering these factors, you can narrow down your options and find the air fryer that best suits your needs and preferences. Remember to keep your cooking habits, kitchen space, and desired features in mind. So, get ready to embark on a flavorful journey and elevate your cooking with the perfect air fryer companion!

What Can You Cook in an Air Fryer and What Foods to Avoid?

The versatility of an air fryer is truly remarkable, as it allows you to cook a wide range of foods with less oil and a crispy, delicious finish. Whether you're a culinary adventurer or a comfort food enthusiast, the possibilities are endless. Let's explore the various dishes you can create in an air fryer and some foods to avoid.

- **Crispy Delights:** Air fryers excel at producing crispy delights without the need for excessive oil. You can enjoy golden and crunchy french fries, onion rings, chicken wings, mozzarella sticks, and even breaded fish or shrimp. The hot air circulating around the food ensures a satisfying crunch while minimising the guilt associated with deep-fried indulgences.
- **Roasted Vegetables:** Roasting vegetables in an air fryer is a game-changer. It brings out their natural sweetness and caramelization, resulting in perfectly roasted Brussels sprouts, cauliflower florets, sweet potato fries, or even a medley of colourful bell peppers. Simply toss the vegetables with a little oil, seasonings of your choice, and let the air fryer work its magic.
- **Grilled Meats and Seafood:** Yes, you read that right! You can achieve that char-grilled flavour on meats and seafood in an air fryer. Marinate chicken drumsticks or skewered kebabs, place them in the air fryer and let the intense heat create a mouthwatering sear. From juicy steaks and grilled salmon fillets to succulent shrimp or even pork chops, the air fryer can deliver satisfying grill-like results.
- **Baked Goods:** Air fryers are not limited to savoury dishes. You can also bake a variety of goods, from muffins and cupcakes to cinnamon rolls and even small cakes. The hot air circulates evenly, ensuring a fluffy and perfectly baked outcome. So, satisfy your sweet tooth with healthier alternatives to traditional baking methods.

While the air fryer opens up a world of culinary possibilities, there are a few foods to avoid or use with caution:

- **Wet Batters:** Foods with wet batters, like tempura or thick pancake batters, may not yield desirable results in an air fryer. The excess moisture can make the food soggy instead of crispy. If you're craving a dish with a wet batter, it's best to stick to traditional deep-frying methods.

- **Delicate Foods:** Delicate foods that require gentle cooking, like flaky fish fillets or tender vegetables, may not fare well in an air fryer. The intense heat and circulating air might cause these foods to become overcooked or dry. It's important to monitor and adjust cooking times accordingly to prevent overcooking.
- **Foods with High Water Content:** Foods with high water content, such as grapes, watery fruits, or leafy greens, are not suitable for air frying. The high moisture content can result in uneven cooking and a less desirable texture. These foods are best enjoyed fresh or prepared using other cooking methods.

Remember, experimentation is key when using an air fryer. Don't be afraid to try new recipes and adapt traditional ones to suit the air fryer's cooking style. With a bit of creativity, you'll discover endless ways to make healthier, flavorful, and crispy meals using this fantastic kitchen appliance.

The Benefits of Air Fryers

Air fryers have taken the culinary world by storm, revolutionising the way we cook our favourite foods. These innovative kitchen appliances offer a healthier alternative to traditional deep frying methods, providing a multitude of benefits that make them a must-have in any kitchen. Let's explore the advantages of using an air fryer and how they can enhance your cooking experience.

- **Healthier Cooking:** One of the most significant benefits of air fryers is their ability to cook food with little to no oil. Traditional deep frying involves submerging food in hot oil, resulting in dishes that are high in unhealthy fats and calories. Air fryers, on the other hand, use hot air circulation to cook food, requiring only a fraction of the oil used in deep frying. This reduction in oil consumption significantly lowers the overall fat content of your favourite dishes, making them a healthier choice for you and your family.

- **Reduced Fat and Calories:** By using significantly less oil, air fryers help you enjoy your favourite fried foods with reduced fat and calorie content. For example, crispy french fries made in an air fryer contain up to 75% less fat compared to traditional deep-fried versions. This reduction in unhealthy fats can contribute to weight management and support a healthier lifestyle without compromising on taste and texture.

- **Crispy and Delicious Results:** Despite using minimal oil, air fryers can achieve that coveted crispy texture that we all love in fried foods. The secret lies in the rapid air circulation within the appliance, which creates a convection effect. This circulating hot air quickly heats the food's surface, producing a crispy exterior while sealing in moisture, resulting in tender and juicy interiors. From crispy chicken wings and golden onion rings to perfectly roasted vegetables, an air fryer can create delicious and satisfying dishes with exceptional texture and flavour.

- **Faster Cooking Time:** Air fryers are known for their speed and efficiency in the kitchen. The intense heat generated by the appliance allows for faster cooking compared to traditional ovens or stovetop methods. The circulating hot air evenly distributes heat, reducing cooking times by up to 20% in some cases. This time-saving benefit is especially valuable for busy individuals or families who want to prepare meals quickly without compromising on taste and quality.

- **Versatility:** Air fryers are incredibly versatile and can be used to cook a wide range of dishes. From appetisers and main courses to desserts and even baked goods, an air fryer can handle it all. You can grill, roast, bake, and even reheat leftovers with ease. The ability to cook various foods in one appliance eliminates the need for multiple cooking tools, saving you valuable kitchen space and simplifying your cooking process.

- **Easy to Use and Clean:** Air fryers are designed to be user-friendly, making them an excellent option for beginners and experienced cooks alike. Most models come with intuitive digital controls, pre-set cooking functions, and adjustable temperature settings, allowing you to easily customise your cooking experience. Additionally, the non-stick surfaces and dishwasher-safe parts make cleaning a breeze, saving you time and effort in the kitchen.

- **Safer Alternative:** Compared to traditional deep frying, air fryers offer a safer cooking method. With no open pots or pans filled with scorching oil, the risk of oil splatters and burns is significantly reduced. Air fryers also come with safety features such as automatic shut-off and cool-touch handles, providing added peace of mind during the cooking process.

Overall, air fryers offer a multitude of benefits that make them a valuable addition to any kitchen. From healthier cooking and reduced fat intake to crispy and delicious results, faster cooking times, versatility, ease of use, and enhanced safety, air fryers have transformed the way we enjoy our favourite foods. By embracing this innovative cooking technology, you can create mouthwatering dishes that satisfy your cravings while promoting a healthier lifestyle.

Cleaning and Maintaining Your Air Fryer

Keeping your air fryer clean and well-maintained is essential for optimal performance and longevity. Regular cleaning not only ensures that your appliance continues to function efficiently but also helps to eliminate any lingering odours and prevent the buildup of grease and residue. Follow these simple steps to clean and maintain your air fryer:
Unplug and Cool Down: Before starting the cleaning process, always ensure that your air fryer is unplugged and has completely cooled down. This will help prevent any accidents or injuries while handling the appliance.

- **Disassemble Removable Parts:** Most air fryers have removable parts that are dishwasher-safe or require hand washing. Check your manufacturer's instructions for specific guidelines. Typically, the removable parts include the frying basket, drip tray, and any other accessories. Carefully detach these components and set them aside for cleaning.

- **Hand Wash or Dishwasher:** If the removable parts are dishwasher-safe, you can place them in the dishwasher for easy cleaning. Otherwise, wash them by hand using warm, soapy water. Use a soft sponge or cloth to gently scrub away any food residue or grease. Rinse thoroughly and allow the parts to air dry, or dry them with a clean towel before reassembling.

- **Clean the Interior:** To clean the interior of your air fryer, use a damp cloth or sponge to wipe away any food particles or oil. Be careful not to immerse the appliance in water or use abrasive cleaners that can damage the surface. If there are stubborn stains or buildup, mix a small amount of dish soap with warm water and gently scrub the affected areas. Wipe dry with a clean cloth.

- **Address Lingering Odours:** If you notice any lingering odours from previous cooking sessions, there are a few simple tricks to freshen up your air fryer. One option is to fill the frying basket with a mixture of water and lemon juice or vinegar and run the air fryer at a low temperature for a few minutes. The steam and acidity will help eliminate odours. Another method is to place a small bowl of baking soda in the air fryer overnight. Baking soda absorbs odours and can leave your appliance smelling fresh.

- **Handle the Exterior:** Wipe the exterior of your air fryer with a damp cloth to remove any grease or fingerprints. If there are stubborn stains or sticky residue, use a mild kitchen cleaner or a mixture of vinegar and water. Avoid using abrasive materials or harsh chemicals that can damage the surface. Dry the exterior with a clean cloth to prevent water spots.

- **Regular Maintenance:** To keep your air fryer in optimal condition, it's important to perform regular maintenance. This includes inspecting the power cord for any signs of damage, ensuring proper ventilation by keeping the air vents clear, and periodically checking for loose screws or any other mechanical issues. Refer to your manufacturer's instructions for any specific maintenance recommendations.

By following these cleaning and maintenance tips, you can enjoy your air fryer for years to come. A clean and well-maintained appliance not only ensures delicious and healthy meals but also keeps your kitchen a safe and pleasant place to cook. So, invest a little time in caring for your air fryer, and it will reward you with exceptional performance and culinary delights.

Care Tips for Your Air Fryer

Taking proper care of your air fryer is essential for its longevity and optimal performance. By following these care tips, you can ensure that your appliance continues to deliver delicious and healthy meals for years to come:

- **Read the Instruction Manual:** Before using your air fryer, make sure to read the instruction manual thoroughly. Each model may have specific care instructions and guidelines that you need to follow. Familiarise yourself with the appliance's features, cleaning recommendations, and any other important information provided by the manufacturer.
- **Use Non-Abrasive Utensils:** When cooking with your air fryer, always use non-abrasive utensils to avoid scratching the non-stick coating of the frying basket or other removable parts. Opt for silicone, wooden, or plastic utensils to protect the surfaces. Avoid metal utensils that can damage the non-stick coating.
- **Preheat the Air Fryer:** Preheating your air fryer before adding food can improve cooking efficiency and results. Most air fryers have a preheating function or require a few minutes of preheating time. Preheating ensures that the cooking chamber reaches the desired temperature and allows for even cooking.

- **Avoid Overcrowding:** To achieve the best cooking results, avoid overcrowding the frying basket. Leave enough space between the food items to allow hot air circulation. Overcrowding can lead to uneven cooking and may prevent the food from becoming crispy. Cook in multiple batches if necessary.
- **Use Parchment Paper or Silicone Liners:** To prevent food from sticking to the frying basket or drip tray, you can use parchment paper or silicone liners. These non-stick liners make cleanup easier and protect the surfaces of the appliance. Make sure the parchment paper or silicone liner is suitable for air fryer use and can withstand high temperatures.
- **Regularly Shake or Flip the Food:** For even cooking and browning, it's recommended to shake or flip the food halfway through the cooking process. This ensures that all sides of the food are exposed to the circulating hot air, resulting in a crispy and evenly cooked outcome. Refer to the recipe or cooking instructions for specific shaking or flipping recommendations.
- **Cool Down Properly:** After cooking, allow your air fryer to cool down completely before cleaning or storing it. Unplug the appliance and let it sit for a while to dissipate any residual heat. This ensures your safety during the cleaning process and prevents any potential damage to the appliance or other surfaces.
- **Store Properly:** When not in use, store your air fryer in a clean and dry place. Make sure it is free from moisture and dust. Store the removable parts separately or place them back in the air fryer if there is enough space. This helps to keep the appliance in good condition and ready for your next cooking adventure.

By following these care tips, you can maintain the quality and performance of your air fryer. Regular cleaning, proper usage, and attention to detail will ensure that your air fryer remains a reliable and versatile kitchen companion. With a well-cared-for appliance, you can continue to enjoy the benefits of healthy and delicious air-fried meals for years to come.

Frequently Asked Questions

Is cooking with an air fryer healthier than traditional frying methods?

Air frying is generally considered a healthier cooking method compared to deep frying. Air fryers use hot air circulation to cook food, requiring little to no oil or only a minimal amount compared to deep frying. This can significantly reduce the overall calorie and fat content of your favourite fried foods.

Can I use aluminium foil or other accessories in the air fryer?

Yes, you can use aluminium foil in your air fryer, but it's important to use it properly. You should create holes in the foil to allow hot air to circulate, ensuring even cooking. Additionally, check the manufacturer's instructions to determine if other accessories, such as baking pans or silicone moulds, are safe to use in your specific air fryer model.

How do I prevent the food from sticking to the air fryer basket?

To prevent food from sticking to the air fryer basket, it's recommended to lightly coat the food with a thin layer of oil or cooking spray before placing it in the basket. Using parchment paper or silicone liners can also help prevent sticking.

Can I cook frozen foods in an air fryer?

Yes, air fryers are excellent for cooking frozen foods. Whether it's frozen fries, chicken nuggets, or vegetables, the air fryer can cook them to crispy perfection. Adjust the cooking time and temperature according to the instructions provided on the food packaging or refer to air fryer cooking guides for frozen foods.

Can I reheat leftovers in the air fryer?

Absolutely! The air fryer is a convenient tool for reheating leftovers. It can help revive the crispiness of fried foods or provide a quick and even reheating for various dishes. Simply place the leftovers in the air fryer basket and heat at a moderate temperature until thoroughly heated.

How do I clean the air fryer?

Cleaning an air fryer is usually straightforward. Start by unplugging the appliance and allowing it to cool down. Remove the removable parts, such as the frying basket and drip tray, and wash them with warm soapy water or place them in the dishwasher if they are dishwasher-safe. Use a non-abrasive sponge or cloth to wipe down the interior and exterior of the air fryer. Be sure to consult the manufacturer's instructions for specific cleaning guidelines.

Can I cook different types of foods simultaneously in the air fryer?

Yes, you can cook different types of foods simultaneously in the air fryer by using dividers or racks designed for your specific model. These accessories help separate the foods, preventing flavours from mingling. However, be mindful of the cooking times and temperatures required for each food item to ensure they cook properly.

Can I use my own recipes in an air fryer?

Absolutely! Air fryers are versatile appliances that can accommodate a wide range of recipes. You can adapt your favourite recipes by adjusting the cooking time and temperature to suit the air fryer's capabilities. Experiment with different dishes and flavours to discover new and exciting ways to use your air fryer.

Crispy Hash Brown Birds' Nests

Serves: 4
Prep time: 10 minutes / Cook time: 18 minutes

Ingredients:
- 400g shredded hash brown potatoes
- 100g shredded cheddar cheese
- 8 cooked breakfast sausage links, chopped
- 4 large eggs
- 60ml whole milk
- 1/4 tsp garlic powder
- 1/4 tsp onion powder
- Salt and black pepper, to taste

Preparation instructions:
1. Preheat the Air Fryer to 190°C for 5 minutes.
2. In a medium bowl, mix together the shredded hash brown potatoes, shredded cheddar cheese, and chopped breakfast sausage links.
3. Divide the mixture evenly among 4 silicone muffin cups, forming nests with a well in the centre.
4. In a separate bowl, whisk together the eggs, whole milk, garlic powder, onion powder, salt, and black pepper.
5. Pour the egg mixture into each hash brown nest until it's 3/4 full.
6. Place the muffin cups in the crisper basket of the Air Fryer and air fry at 190°C for 18 minutes or until the hash browns are golden brown and the eggs are set.
7. Once cooked, remove the nests from the Air Fryer and let them cool for a few minutes before serving. Serve hot.

Savory Stuffed Bell Pepper Omelette Bombs

Serves: 4
Prep time: 10 minutes / Cook time: 18 minutes

Ingredients:
- 4 bell peppers (any colour), tops removed and seeded
- 4 slices cooked bacon, crumbled
- 100g shredded cheddar cheese
- 4 large eggs
- 60ml whole milk
- 1/4 tsp garlic powder
- 1/4 tsp onion powder
- Salt and black pepper, to taste
- Fresh chives, for garnish (optional)

Preparation instructions:
1. Preheat the Air Fryer to 190°C for 5 minutes.
2. In a bowl, combine the crumbled bacon and shredded cheddar cheese.
3. Stuff each bell pepper with the bacon and cheese mixture.
4. In a separate bowl, whisk together the eggs, whole milk, garlic powder, onion powder, salt, and black pepper.
5. Pour the egg mixture into each stuffed bell pepper until it's almost full.
6. Place the bell peppers in the crisper basket of the Air Fryer and air fry at 190°C for 18 minutes or until the eggs are fully cooked and set.
7. Once cooked, remove the bell peppers from the Air Fryer and let them cool slightly. Garnish with fresh chives, if desired, before serving. Enjoy!

Maple Glazed Bacon Cinnamon Rolls

Serves: 4
Prep time: 10 minutes / Cook time: 18 minutes

Ingredients:
- 1 can (400g) refrigerated cinnamon rolls
- 8 slices bacon, cooked until crispy
- 60ml maple syrup
- 30g chopped pecans (optional)

Preparation instructions:
1. Preheat the Air Fryer to 190°C for 5 minutes.
2. Separate the individual cinnamon rolls from the can and set the icing aside.
3. Wrap each cinnamon roll tightly with a slice of cooked bacon.
4. Place the bacon-wrapped cinnamon rolls in the crisper basket of the Air Fryer.
5. Drizzle the maple syrup over the rolls and sprinkle with chopped pecans, if using.
6. Air fry at 190°C for 18 minutes or until the cinnamon rolls are golden brown and cooked through.

7. Once cooked, remove the rolls from the Air Fryer and let them cool slightly. Drizzle the reserved icing from the can over the warm rolls before serving. Enjoy!

Cheesy Spinach and Artichoke Frittata Muffins

Serves: 4
Prep time: 10 minutes / Cook time: 18 minutes

Ingredients:
- 4 large eggs
- 60ml whole milk
- 50g shredded cheddar cheese
- 50g shredded mozzarella cheese
- 50g chopped spinach, cooked and squeezed dry
- 50g canned artichoke hearts, drained and chopped
- 1/4 tsp garlic powder
- 1/4 tsp onion powder
- Salt and black pepper, to taste

Preparation instructions:
1. Preheat the Air Fryer to 190°C for 5 minutes.
2. In a bowl, whisk together the eggs, whole milk, shredded cheddar cheese, shredded mozzarella cheese, chopped spinach, chopped artichoke hearts, garlic powder, onion powder, salt, and black pepper.
3. Divide the mixture evenly among 4 silicone muffin cups.
4. Place the muffin cups in the crisper basket of the Air Fryer and air fry at 190°C for 18 minutes or until the frittata muffins are set and lightly golden on top.
5. Once cooked, remove the muffins from the Air Fryer and let them cool for a few minutes before serving. Enjoy these delicious frittata muffins!

Pesto and Sun-Dried Tomato Egg Bites

Serves: 4
Prep time: 10 minutes / Cook time: 18 minutes

Ingredients:
- 4 large eggs
- 60ml whole milk
- 2 tbsp pesto sauce
- 30g chopped sun-dried tomatoes
- 30g crumbled feta cheese
- Salt and black pepper, to taste
- Fresh basil leaves, for garnish (optional)

Preparation instructions:
1. Preheat the Air Fryer to 190°C for 5 minutes.
2. In a bowl, whisk together the eggs, whole milk, pesto sauce, chopped sun-dried tomatoes, crumbled feta cheese, salt, and black pepper.
3. Divide the mixture evenly among 4 silicone muffin cups.
4. Place the muffin cups in the crisper basket of the Air Fryer and air fry at 190°C for 18 minutes or until the egg bites are set and lightly golden on top.
5. Once cooked, remove the egg bites from the Air Fryer and let them cool for a few minutes. Garnish with fresh basil leaves, if desired, before serving. Enjoy these flavorful egg bites!

Sweet Potato and Black Bean Breakfast Tacos

Serves: 4
Prep time: 15 minutes / Cook time: 12 minutes

Ingredients:
- 2 medium sweet potatoes, peeled and diced
- 1 tbsp olive oil
- 1/2 tsp ground cumin
- 1/2 tsp paprika
- 1/4 tsp chilli powder
- Salt and black pepper, to taste
- 200g canned black beans, rinsed and drained
- 4 large eggs
- 60ml whole milk
- 4 small tortilla wraps
- 50g shredded cheddar cheese
- Fresh cilantro, for garnish (optional)
- Salsa or hot sauce, for serving (optional)

Preparation instructions:
1. Preheat the Air Fryer to 200°C for 5 minutes.
2. In a bowl, toss the diced sweet potatoes with olive oil, ground cumin, paprika, chilli powder, salt, and black pepper.
3. Place the seasoned sweet potatoes in the Air Fryer basket and air fry at 200°C for 12 minutes or until they are tender and slightly crispy.
4. In the meantime, in a separate bowl, whisk together the eggs and whole milk. Season with salt and black pepper.
5. Pour the egg mixture into a greased Air Fryer-safe pan and cook at 180°C for 5 minutes or until the eggs are cooked through. Slice into strips.

6. Warm the tortilla wraps in the Air Fryer for 1-2 minutes.
7. Assemble the breakfast tacos by filling each tortilla with the cooked sweet potatoes, black beans, scrambled eggs, shredded cheddar cheese, and fresh cilantro.
8. Serve the tacos with salsa or hot sauce, if desired. Enjoy these delicious sweet potato and black bean breakfast tacos!

Blueberry-Lemon Ricotta Pancake Poppers

Serves: 4
Prep time: 10 minutes / Cook time: 8 minutes

Ingredients:

* 100g ricotta cheese
* 2 large eggs
* 60ml whole milk
* 1 tbsp melted butter
* 50g all-purpose flour
* 1 tbsp granulated sugar
* 1/2 tsp baking powder
* 1/4 tsp lemon zest
* 50g fresh blueberries
* Icing sugar, for dusting
* Maple syrup, for serving

Preparation instructions:

1. Preheat the Air Fryer to 180°C for 5 minutes.
2. In a bowl, whisk together the ricotta cheese, eggs, whole milk, melted butter, all-purpose flour, granulated sugar, baking powder, and lemon zest until smooth.
3. Gently fold in the fresh blueberries.
4. Fill a greased silicone mini muffin pan with the pancake batter, filling each cavity about 3/4 full.
5. Place the muffin pan in the Air Fryer basket and air fry at 180°C for 8 minutes or until the pancake poppers are golden brown and cooked through.
6. Once cooked, remove the pancake poppers from the Air Fryer and let them cool for a few minutes.
7. Dust with icing sugar and serve with maple syrup. Enjoy these delightful blueberry-lemon ricotta pancake poppers!

Zucchini and Goat Cheese Egg White Wraps

Serves: 4
Prep time: 10 minutes / Cook time: 8 minutes

Ingredients:

* 4 large egg whites
* 60ml whole milk
* Salt and black pepper, to taste
* 1 tsp olive oil
* 1 small zucchini, grated and excess moisture squeezed out
* 30g crumbled goat cheese
* Fresh basil leaves, for garnish (optional)

Preparation instructions:

1. Preheat the Air Fryer to 180°C for 5 minutes.
2. In a bowl, whisk together the egg whites, whole milk, salt, and black pepper.
3. Heat the olive oil in a skillet over medium heat. Add the grated zucchini and sauté for 2-3 minutes until it softens.
4. Pour the egg white mixture into the skillet with the zucchini. Cook, stirring occasionally, until the eggs are fully cooked and scrambled.
5. Divide the scrambled eggs and zucchini mixture among 4 small tortilla wraps.
6. Sprinkle crumbled goat cheese over the wraps and garnish with fresh basil leaves, if desired.
7. Place the wraps in the Air Fryer basket and air fry at 180°C for 8 minutes or until the wraps are crispy and heated through.
8. Once cooked, remove the wraps from the Air Fryer and serve. Enjoy these flavorful zucchini and goat cheese egg white wraps!

Caramelized Onion and Mushroom Breakfast Quesadillas

Serves: 4
Prep time: 10 minutes / Cook time: 15 minutes

Ingredients:

* 1 tbsp olive oil
* 1 medium onion, thinly sliced
* 200g mushrooms, sliced
* Salt and black pepper, to taste
* 4 large tortilla wraps
* 100g shredded cheddar cheese
* 4 large eggs
* 60ml whole milk
* Fresh parsley, for garnish (optional)
* Sour cream or salsa, for serving (optional)

Preparation instructions:

1. Preheat the Air Fryer to 180°C for 5 minutes.

2. Heat the olive oil in a skillet over medium heat. Add the sliced onion and mushrooms. Sauté for 8-10 minutes, stirring occasionally, until the onions and mushrooms are caramelised and golden brown. Season with salt and black pepper.
3. Place a tortilla wrap on a flat surface. Sprinkle a portion of shredded cheddar cheese on one half of the tortilla.
4. Spread a portion of the caramelised onion and mushroom mixture on top of the cheese.
5. In a bowl, whisk together the eggs, whole milk, salt, and black pepper. Pour a portion of the egg mixture over the onion and mushroom layer.
6. Fold the tortilla in half to cover the filling, creating a quesadilla.
7. Repeat steps 3-6 for the remaining tortilla wraps and filling.
8. Place the quesadillas in the Air Fryer basket and air fry at 180°C for 15 minutes or until the quesadillas are crispy and the eggs are fully cooked.
9. Once cooked, remove the quesadillas from the Air Fryer and let them cool slightly. Garnish with fresh parsley, if desired.
10. Serve the quesadillas with sour cream or salsa, if desired. Enjoy these delicious caramelised onion and mushroom breakfast quesadillas!

Chicken and Waffle Sliders with Sriracha Honey Butter

Serves: 4
Prep time: 10 minutes / Cook time: 10 minutes

Ingredients:
* 4 small chicken breast fillets
* Salt and black pepper, to taste
* 1/2 tsp garlic powder
* 1/2 tsp paprika
* 1/4 tsp cayenne pepper
* 4 frozen mini waffles
* 60g unsalted butter, softened
* 1 tbsp honey
* 1 tsp sriracha sauce (adjust to taste)
* Fresh chives, for garnish (optional)

Preparation instructions:
1. Preheat the Air Fryer to 200°C for 5 minutes.
2. Season the chicken breast fillets with salt, black pepper, garlic powder, paprika, and cayenne pepper.
3. Place the seasoned chicken breast fillets in the Air

Fryer basket and air fry at 200°C for 10 minutes or until the chicken is cooked through and golden brown. Flip halfway through cooking.
4. In the meantime, cook the mini waffles according to the package instructions.
5. In a small bowl, combine the softened butter, honey, and sriracha sauce. Mix well until smooth and creamy.
6. Slice the cooked chicken breast fillets into smaller pieces to fit the size of the mini waffles.
7. Spread a generous amount of the sriracha honey butter on each mini waffle.
8. Place a piece of chicken on one mini waffle and sandwich it with another mini waffle, butter side down.
9. Repeat for the remaining waffles and chicken.
10. Place the sliders in the Air Fryer basket and air fry at 180°C for 2-3 minutes or until the waffles are crispy and heated through.
11. Once cooked, remove the sliders from the Air Fryer and garnish with fresh chives, if desired. Serve these tasty chicken and waffle sliders with sriracha honey butter!

Spinach and Feta Stuffed French Toast Roll-Ups

Serves: 4
Prep time: 15 minutes / Cook time: 8 minutes

Ingredients:
* 4 slices white bread
* 60g cream cheese, softened
* 50g frozen chopped spinach, thawed and squeezed dry
* 50g crumbled feta cheese
* 1/4 tsp garlic powder
* 1/4 tsp onion powder
* 2 large eggs
* 60ml whole milk
* 1 tbsp butter, melted
* Maple syrup, for serving

Preparation instructions:
1. Preheat the Air Fryer to 180°C for 5 minutes.
2. Trim the crusts off the bread slices and flatten them with a rolling pin.
3. In a bowl, mix together the cream cheese, chopped spinach, crumbled feta cheese, garlic powder, and onion powder until well combined.

4. Spread a portion of the cream cheese mixture evenly onto each flattened bread slice.
5. Roll up each bread slice tightly, like a cigar, and set aside.
6. In a shallow bowl, whisk together the eggs, whole milk, and melted butter.
7. Dip each rolled bread slice into the egg mixture, making sure it is fully coated.
8. Place the stuffed and rolled French toast in the Air Fryer basket and air fry at 180°C for 8 minutes or until the roll-ups are golden brown and crispy.
9. Once cooked, remove the French toast roll-ups from the Air Fryer and let them cool slightly before serving.
10. Serve the spinach and feta stuffed French toast roll-ups with maple syrup for dipping. Enjoy these delightful and savoury breakfast treats!

Crispy Prosciutto and Brie Breakfast Pizza

Serves: 4
Prep time: 10 minutes / Cook time: 10 minutes

Ingredients:
- 1 pre-made pizza dough (about 300g)
- 60ml pizza sauce
- 100g brie cheese, sliced
- 50g baby spinach leaves
- 4 slices prosciutto
- Fresh basil leaves, for garnish (optional)

Preparation instructions:
1. Preheat the Air Fryer to 200°C for 5 minutes.
2. Roll out the pizza dough into a circle or desired shape.
3. Spread the pizza sauce evenly over the dough, leaving a small border around the edges.
4. Arrange the sliced brie cheese on top of the sauce.
5. Add the baby spinach leaves, distributing them evenly.
6. Tear the prosciutto slices into smaller pieces and scatter them over the pizza.
7. Place the pizza in the Air Fryer basket and air fry at 200°C for 10 minutes or until the crust is crispy and golden brown, and the cheese is melted and bubbly.
8. Once cooked, remove the pizza from the Air Fryer and let it cool for a few minutes. Garnish with fresh basil leaves, if desired.

9. Slice the crispy prosciutto and brie breakfast pizza and serve hot. Enjoy this delicious and savoury breakfast pizza!

Apple Cinnamon Quinoa Breakfast Bowls

Serves: 4
Prep time: 10 minutes / Cook time: 20 minutes

Ingredients:
- 100g quinoa
- 240ml water
- 240ml whole milk
- 2 tbsp maple syrup
- 1/2 tsp ground cinnamon
- 1/4 tsp vanilla extract
- 2 apples, peeled, cored, and chopped
- 30g chopped walnuts
- Fresh apple slices, for garnish (optional)
- Greek yoghurt or milk, for serving (optional)

Preparation instructions:
1. Rinse the quinoa under cold water using a fine-mesh sieve.
2. In a saucepan, combine the rinsed quinoa, water, whole milk, maple syrup, ground cinnamon, and vanilla extract.
3. Bring the mixture to a boil over medium-high heat, then reduce the heat to low, cover, and simmer for 15-20 minutes or until the quinoa is cooked and the liquid is absorbed. Stir occasionally.
4. While the quinoa is cooking, preheat the Air Fryer to 180°C for 5 minutes.
5. In a separate bowl, toss the chopped apples with a sprinkle of cinnamon.
6. Place the cinnamon-coated apples in the Air Fryer basket and air fry at 180°C for 8-10 minutes or until they are tender and slightly caramelised, stirring halfway through.
7. Once the quinoa is cooked, fluff it with a fork and divide it into serving bowls.
8. Top each bowl of quinoa with the sautéed apples and chopped walnuts.
9. Garnish with fresh apple slices, if desired.
10. Serve the apple cinnamon quinoa breakfast bowls with a dollop of Greek yoghurt or a splash of milk, if desired. Enjoy these nutritious and flavorful breakfast bowls made using your Air Fryer!

Lemon Poppy Seed Pancake Bites with Blueberry Compote

Serves: 4
Prep time: 10 minutes / Cook time: 8 minutes

Ingredients:

- 150g all-purpose flour
- 1 tbsp granulated sugar
- 1/2 tsp baking powder
- 1/4 tsp baking soda
- 1/4 tsp salt
- 1 tbsp poppy seeds
- 240ml buttermilk
- 1 large egg
- 1 tbsp melted butter
- 1 tbsp lemon juice
- 1 tsp lemon zest
- For the Blueberry Compote:
- 200g fresh blueberries
- 2 tbsp water
- 1 tbsp granulated sugar
- 1 tsp lemon juice

Preparation instructions:

1. Preheat the Air Fryer to 180°C for 5 minutes.
2. In a bowl, whisk together the flour, sugar, baking powder, baking soda, salt, and poppy seeds.
3. In a separate bowl, whisk together the buttermilk, egg, melted butter, lemon juice, and lemon zest.
4. Pour the wet Ingredients into the dry Ingredients and mix until just combined. Do not overmix.
5. Grease a silicone mini muffin pan and spoon the pancake batter into each cavity, filling them about 3/4 full.
6. Place the muffin pan in the Air Fryer basket and air fry at 180°C for 8 minutes or until the pancake bites are golden brown and cooked through.
7. While the pancake bites are cooking, prepare the blueberry compote. In a small saucepan, combine the blueberries, water, granulated sugar, and lemon juice. Simmer over low heat for about 5 minutes, stirring occasionally, until the blueberries break down and the sauce thickens slightly.
8. Once the pancake bites are cooked, remove them from the Air Fryer and let them cool for a few minutes.
9. Serve the lemon poppy seed pancake bites with the blueberry compote drizzled on top. Enjoy these delightful pancake bites with a burst of lemony flavour and sweet blueberry compote!

Peanut Butter and Jelly Stuffed French Toast Bites

Serves: 4
Prep time: 15 minutes / Cook time: 8 minutes

Ingredients:

- 8 slices white bread
- 120g creamy peanut butter
- 80g strawberry or grape jelly
- 2 large eggs
- 60ml whole milk
- 1/2 tsp vanilla extract
- 1/4 tsp ground cinnamon
- 2 tbsp unsalted butter
- Powdered sugar, for dusting (optional)
- Maple syrup, for serving

Preparation instructions:

1. Preheat the Air Fryer to 180°C for 5 minutes.
2. Spread peanut butter on one side of 4 bread slices, and jelly on one side of the other 4 bread slices.
3. Place one peanut butter slice together with one jelly slice to form a sandwich. Repeat for the remaining slices.
4. Cut each sandwich into bite-sized squares or triangles.
5. In a shallow bowl, whisk together the eggs, whole milk, vanilla extract, and ground cinnamon.
6. Dip each peanut butter and jelly sandwich bite into the egg mixture, coating both sides evenly.
7. Melt the unsalted butter in a skillet over medium heat. Add the coated sandwich bites and cook for 2-3 minutes on each side until golden brown.
8. Once cooked, transfer the French toast bites to the Air Fryer basket and air fry at 180°C for an additional 3-4 minutes or until they are crispy and heated through.
9. Remove the French toast bites from the Air Fryer and dust with powdered sugar, if desired.
10. Serve the peanut butter and jelly stuffed French toast bites with maple syrup for dipping. Enjoy these delightful and nostalgic breakfast bites!

Blackberry Cobbler

Serves: 6
Prep time: 15 minutes / Cook time: 25-30 minutes

Ingredients

- 375 g fresh or frozen blackberries
- 220 g sugar, divided
- 1 teaspoon vanilla extract
- 8 tablespoons butter, melted
- 125 g self-raising flour
- 1 to 2 tablespoons oil

Preparation instructions

1. In a medium bowl, stir together the blackberries, 125 g sugar, and vanilla
2. In another medium bowl, stir together the melted butter, remaining 95 g sugar, and flour until a dough forms.
3. Spritz a baking pan with oil. Add the blackberry mixture. Crumble the flour mixture over the fruit. Cover the pan with aluminum foil.
4. Preheat the air fryer to 176°C.
5. Place the covered pan in the air fryer basket. Cook for 20 to 25 minutes until the filling is thickened.
6. Uncover the pan and cook for 5 minutes more, depending on how juicy and browned you like your cobbler. Let sit for 5 minutes before serving.

Strawberry Banana Bread

Serves: 2-4 people
Prep time: 20 minutes | Cook time: 40-45 minutes

Ingredients

- 200g all-purpose flour
- 5g baking powder
- 2 ripe bananas, mashed
- 100g strawberries, diced
- 100g granulated sugar
- 50g unsalted butter, melted
- 30 ml milk
- 1 egg
- 5 ml vanilla extract

Preparation instructions

1. Preheat the air fryer to 160°C (320°F).
2. In a bowl, combine the all-purpose flour and baking powder. Set aside.
3. In a separate bowl, mix together the mashed bananas, diced strawberries, granulated sugar, melted butter, milk, egg, and vanilla extract until well-combined.
4. Gradually add the dry Ingredients to the wet Ingredients and mix until just combined. Do not overmix.

5. Pour the batter into a greased and lined loaf pan that fits inside the air fryer basket.
6. Place the loaf pan in the air fryer basket and air fry for 40-45 minutes, or until a toothpick inserted into the centre comes out clean.
7. Remove the pan from the air fryer and let the bread cool before slicing and serving.

Cheesy Air Fryer Garlic Bread

Serves: 2-4 people
Prep time: 10 minutes | Cook time: 6-8 minutes

Ingredients

- 1 loaf of French bread, sliced in half lengthwise
- 60g unsalted butter, softened
- 5g garlic powder
- 5g dried parsley
- 100g shredded mozzarella cheese

Preparation instructions:

1. Preheat the air fryer to 180°C (350°F).
2. In a small bowl, combine the softened butter, garlic powder, and dried parsley. Mix well to create a garlic butter spread.
3. Spread the garlic butter evenly on the cut sides of the French bread.
4. Sprinkle the shredded mozzarella cheese on top of the garlic butter.
5. Place the bread, cut side up, in the air fryer basket.
6. Air fry for 6-8 minutes, or until the cheese is melted and bubbly, and the bread is toasted to your desired level of crispness.
7. Remove from the air fryer, slice, and serve hot as a delightful side dish or appetiser.

Mozzarella Sticks with Marinara Sauce

Serves: 2 people
Prep time: 10-15 minutes | Cook time: 8 minutes

Ingredients

- 200g mozzarella cheese sticks, cut in half
- 2 eggs, beaten
- 60g breadcrumbs
- 5g Italian seasoning
- 5g garlic powder
- 30g grated Parmesan cheese
- Cooking spray
- Marinara sauce (for serving)

Preparation instructions:

1. Preheat the air fryer to 200°C (400°F).
2. Dip each mozzarella stick half into the beaten eggs, allowing any excess to drip off.
3. In a shallow dish, combine the breadcrumbs, Italian seasoning, garlic powder, and grated Parmesan cheese.
4. Roll each mozzarella stick half in the breadcrumb mixture, pressing lightly to adhere.
5. Place the coated mozzarella sticks in a single layer in the air fryer basket, leaving space between them.
6. Lightly spray the mozzarella sticks with cooking spray.
7. Air fry for 6-8 minutes, or until the cheese is melted and the coating is golden brown and crispy.
8. Remove from the air fryer and let them cool for a few minutes.
9. Serve the mozzarella sticks hot with marinara sauce for dipping.

Full English Breakfast

Serves: 2-4 people
Prep time: 10-15 minutes | Cook time: 20-25 minutes

Ingredients:

- 4 slices of bacon
- 4 breakfast sausages
- 4 medium-sized eggs
- 2 medium-sized tomatoes, sliced
- 4 slices of bread
- 1 can of baked beans
- Salt and pepper to taste
- Optional: mushrooms, black pudding, or hash browns

Preparation instructions:

1. Preheat the air fryer to 180°C (350°F).
2. Place the bacon and sausages in the air fryer basket and cook for 10-12 minutes, flipping halfway through, until crispy and cooked through.
3. Remove the bacon and sausages from the air fryer and place on a plate lined with paper towels to drain excess oil.
4. Add the sliced tomatoes to the air fryer basket and cook for 5-7 minutes until softened and slightly charred.

5. Toast the bread slices in a toaster or air fryer until golden brown and crispy.
6. In a saucepan, heat up the baked beans over medium heat until hot.
7. Crack the eggs into a bowl, season with salt and pepper, and whisk well.
8. Pour the beaten eggs into the air fryer basket and cook for 3-5 minutes or until set.
9. Optional: add sliced mushrooms or hash browns to the air fryer basket and cook for an additional 5-7 minutes, until golden brown.
10. Serve the cooked bacon, sausages, tomatoes, and eggs on a plate with the toasted bread slices and hot baked beans on the side. Optional: serve with black pudding or other breakfast items of your choice. Enjoy your delicious and satisfying Full English Breakfast!

Pumpkin Pudding with Vanilla Wafers

Serves: 4
Prep time: 10 minutes | Cook time: 12-17 minutes

Ingredients

- 250 g canned no-salt-added pumpkin purée (not pumpkin pie filling)
- 50 g packed brown sugar
- 3 tablespoons plain flour
- 1 egg, whisked
- 2 tablespoons milk
- 1 tablespoon unsalted butter, melted
- 1 teaspoon pure vanilla extract
- 4 low-fat vanilla, or plain wafers, crumbled
- Nonstick cooking spray

Preparation instructions

1. Preheat the air fryer to 176ºC. Coat a baking pan with nonstick cooking spray. Set aside.
2. Mix the pumpkin purée, brown sugar, flour, whisked egg, milk, melted butter, and vanilla in a medium bowl and whisk to combine. Transfer the mixture to the baking pan.
3. Place the baking pan in the air fryer basket and bake for 12 to 17 minutes until set. 4. Remove the pudding from the basket to a wire rack to cool.
4. Divide the pudding into four bowls and serve with the vanilla wafers sprinkled on top.

Crispy Bacon and Egg Pie Recipe

Serves: 4 people
Prep time: 10 minutes | Cook time: 20 minutes

Ingredients:

- 6 slices bacon, chopped
- 2 tbsp butter
- 4 eggs
- 60 ml milk
- Salt and pepper to taste
- 30g grated cheddar cheese
- 1 refrigerated pie crust

Preparation instructions:

1. Preheat the air fryer at 375°F for 5 minutes.
2. In a pan, cook chopped bacon until crispy. Remove from heat and set aside.
3. In a bowl, whisk together eggs, milk, salt and pepper until well blended. Stir in grated cheese and cooked bacon.
4. Roll out the refrigerated pie crust and cut into 4 equal pieces. Place each piece in a greased air fryer basket.
5. Pour the egg mixture evenly into each pie crust.
6. Air fry for 15-20 minutes or until golden brown and the eggs are set.
7. Serve hot and enjoy your crispy bacon and egg pie!

Devilled Kidneys Recipe

Serves: 2
Prep time: 10 minutes | Cook time: 8 minutes

Ingredients:

- 4 lamb kidneys, trimmed and halved
- 1/2 teaspoon cayenne pepper
- 1/2 teaspoon English mustard
- 1 tablespoon Worcestershire sauce
- 1/2 tablespoon tomato ketchup
- 1/4 teaspoon salt
- 1/4 teaspoon black pepper
- 3 tablespoons unsalted butter, melted
- 1 tablespoon plain flour
- 60ml beef stock
- 2 slices of bread, toasted
- Chopped parsley, to garnish

Preparation instructions:

1. Preheat the air fryer to 200°C.
2. In a small bowl, combine the cayenne pepper, English mustard, Worcestershire sauce, tomato ketchup, salt, black pepper, and melted butter.
3. Add the halved lamb kidneys and toss to coat evenly.
4. Place the kidneys in the air fryer basket and cook for 6 minutes.
5. In a separate bowl, mix the flour and beef stock together.
6. After 6 minutes, remove the kidneys from the air fryer and pour the beef stock mixture over them.
7. Return the kidneys to the air fryer and cook for an additional 2 minutes.
8. Serve the devilled kidneys hot with toasted bread and chopped parsley.

Shropshire Fidget Pie

Serves: 4
Prep time: 25 minutes | Cook time: 40 minutes

Ingredients:

- 500g potatoes, peeled and sliced
- 1 onion, finely chopped
- 200g smoked bacon, diced
- 2 apples, peeled and sliced
- 100ml chicken stock
- Salt and pepper to taste
- 1/2 tsp dried sage
- 1/2 tsp dried thyme
- 1 sheet of puff pastry
- 1 egg, beaten

Preparation instructions:

1. Preheat the air fryer to 180°C.
2. In a large bowl, mix together the potatoes, onion, bacon, apples, chicken stock, salt, pepper, sage, and thyme.
3. Transfer the mixture into the air fryer basket and cook for 20 minutes, stirring occasionally.
4. Roll out the puff pastry sheet to fit the size of your air fryer basket.
5. Place the cooked potato mixture onto the pastry.
6. Brush the edges of the pastry with beaten egg.
7. Cover the pie with the remaining pastry and press the edges together to seal.
8. Brush the top of the pastry with beaten egg.
9. 0Cook the pie in the air fryer for another 20 minutes or until the pastry is golden brown.
10. Serve hot.

Chapter 2: Main Recipes

Cajun Stuffed Bell Peppers

Serves: 4
Prep time: 15 minutes / Cook time: 20 minutes

Ingredients:
- 4 large bell peppers
- 200g cooked rice
- 200g cooked andouille sausage, chopped
- 150g cooked chicken breast, shredded
- 1 small onion, diced
- 1 celery stalk, diced
- 1 red bell pepper, diced
- 1 green bell pepper, diced
- 2 cloves garlic, minced
- 2 tbsp Cajun seasoning
- 1 tbsp olive oil
- Salt and black pepper, to taste
- Fresh parsley, for garnish

Preparation instructions:
1. Preheat the Air Fryer to 180°C for 5 minutes.
2. Cut the tops off the bell peppers and remove the seeds and membranes. Set aside.
3. In a large bowl, combine the cooked rice, chopped andouille sausage, shredded chicken breast, diced onion, diced celery, diced red bell pepper, diced green bell pepper, minced garlic, Cajun seasoning, olive oil, salt, and black pepper. Mix well to combine.
4. Stuff each bell pepper with the Cajun rice and meat mixture, pressing it down gently to fill the cavity.
5. Place the stuffed bell peppers in the Air Fryer basket and air fry at 180°C for 18-20 minutes or until the bell peppers are tender and slightly charred.
6. Once cooked, remove the Cajun stuffed bell peppers from the Air Fryer and let them cool for a few minutes.
7. Garnish with fresh parsley and serve hot. Enjoy these flavorful and spicy Cajun stuffed bell peppers!

Chimichurri Marinated Steak with Roasted Vegetables

Serves: 4
Prep time: 15 minutes + marinating time / Cook time: 20 minutes

Ingredients:
For the Chimichurri Marinade:
- 60ml olive oil
- 60ml red wine vinegar
- 70g fresh parsley leaves, chopped
- 4 cloves garlic, minced
- 1 tsp dried oregano
- 1/2 tsp red pepper flakes
- Salt and black pepper, to taste

For the Steak and Roasted Vegetables:
- 4 beef steaks (sirloin, ribeye, or your preferred cut)
- 600g mixed vegetables (such as bell peppers, zucchini, and red onion), cut into chunks
- 2 tbsp olive oil
- Salt and black pepper, to taste

Preparation instructions:
1. In a bowl, whisk together the olive oil, red wine vinegar, chopped parsley, minced garlic, dried oregano, red pepper flakes, salt, and black pepper to make the chimichurri marinade.
2. Place the steaks in a shallow dish and pour the chimichurri marinade over them. Make sure the steaks are well coated. Cover and refrigerate for at least 1 hour or overnight for better flavour infusion.
3. Preheat the Air Fryer to 200°C for 5 minutes.
4. In a separate bowl, toss the mixed vegetables with olive oil, salt, and black pepper until well coated.
5. Spread the vegetables in a single layer in the Air Fryer basket.
6. Remove the steaks from the marinade, allowing any excess marinade to drip off. Place the steaks in the Air Fryer basket alongside the vegetables.
7. Air fry at 200°C for 10 minutes for medium-rare steaks, or adjust the time according to your desired doneness.

8. After 10 minutes, flip the steaks and toss the vegetables. Air fry for an additional 8-10 minutes or until the steaks are cooked to your liking and the vegetables are tender and slightly charred.

9. Once cooked, remove the steak and roasted vegetables from the Air Fryer and let the steaks rest for a few minutes before slicing.

10. Serve the sliced chimichurri-marinated steak with the roasted vegetables. Enjoy this delicious and vibrant dish!

Garlic Parmesan Pork Chops with Roasted Brussels Sprouts

Serves: 4
Prep time: 10 minutes / Cook time: 20 minutes

Ingredients:
For the Pork Chops:
- 4 boneless pork chops
- 2 cloves garlic, minced
- 2 tbsp grated Parmesan cheese
- 1 tsp dried thyme
- 1/2 tsp garlic powder
- 1/2 tsp onion powder
- Salt and black pepper, to taste

For the Roasted Brussels Sprouts:
- 500g Brussels sprouts, trimmed and halved
- 2 tbsp olive oil
- 2 cloves garlic, minced
- 2 tbsp grated Parmesan cheese
- Salt and black pepper, to taste

Preparation instructions:
1. Preheat the Air Fryer to 200°C for 5 minutes.

2. In a small bowl, combine the minced garlic, grated Parmesan cheese, dried thyme, garlic powder, onion powder, salt, and black pepper to make the seasoning for the pork chops.

3. Pat the pork chops dry with a paper towel and rub the seasoning mixture onto both sides of the chops.

4. Place the pork chops in the Air Fryer basket and air fry at 200°C for 10 minutes.

5. While the pork chops are cooking, in a separate bowl, toss the halved Brussels sprouts with olive oil, minced garlic, grated Parmesan cheese, salt, and black pepper until well coated.

6. After 10 minutes, add the Brussels sprouts to the Air Fryer basket with the pork chops.

7. Air fry at 200°C for an additional 8-10 minutes or until the pork chops are cooked through and the Brussels sprouts are tender and lightly browned.

8. Once cooked, remove the pork chops and Brussels sprouts from the Air Fryer and let them rest for a few minutes.

9. Serve the garlic Parmesan pork chops with the roasted Brussels sprouts. Enjoy this delicious and satisfying meal!

Teriyaki Glazed Salmon with Sesame Broccoli

Serves: 4
Prep time: 10 minutes / Cook time: 15 minutes

Ingredients:
- For the Teriyaki Glaze:
- 80 ml soy sauce
- 60ml water
- 2 tbsp honey or maple syrup
- 2 tbsp rice vinegar
- 1 clove garlic, minced
- 1 tsp grated ginger
- 1 tsp cornstarch
- For the Salmon and Sesame Broccoli:
- 4 salmon fillets
- 500g broccoli florets
- 2 tbsp olive oil
- 2 tbsp sesame seeds
- Salt and black pepper, to taste
- Sliced green onions, for garnish

Preparation instructions:
1. In a saucepan, combine the soy sauce, water, honey or maple syrup, rice vinegar, minced garlic, grated ginger, and cornstarch. Whisk together until the cornstarch is dissolved.

2. Place the saucepan over medium heat and bring the mixture to a simmer. Cook for 2-3 minutes or until the sauce thickens. Remove from heat and set aside.

3. Preheat the Air Fryer to 180°C for 5 minutes.

4. Place the salmon fillets in the Air Fryer basket and brush them generously with the prepared teriyaki glaze.

5. Toss the broccoli florets with olive oil, sesame seeds, salt, and black pepper in a separate bowl

until well coated.

6. Add the sesame-coated broccoli to the Air Fryer basket alongside the salmon fillets.

7. Air fry at 180°C for 12-15 minutes or until the salmon is cooked through and the broccoli is tender-crisp, with a slight char.

9. Once cooked, remove the salmon and sesame broccoli from the Air Fryer.

10. Serve the teriyaki glazed salmon with the sesame broccoli. Garnish with sliced green onions. Enjoy this flavorful and healthy dish!

Crispy Buttermilk Fried Chicken with Honey Mustard Sauce

Serves: 4
Prep time: 20 minutes + marinating time / Cook time: 25 minutes

Ingredients:
For the Fried Chicken:
- 4 chicken leg quarters, separated into drumsticks and thighs
- 300ml buttermilk
- 200g all-purpose flour
- 1 tsp paprika
- 1 tsp garlic powder
- 1 tsp onion powder
- 1/2 tsp dried thyme
- 1/2 tsp dried oregano
- 1/2 tsp salt
- 1/4 tsp black pepper
- Vegetable oil, for frying

For the Honey Mustard Sauce:
- 60ml mayonnaise
- 2 tbsp Dijon mustard
- 2 tbsp honey
- 1 tbsp lemon juice
- Salt and black pepper, to taste

Preparation instructions:
1. In a bowl, marinate the chicken leg quarters in buttermilk. Cover and refrigerate for at least 2 hours or overnight for better flavour.

2. In a shallow dish, combine the all-purpose flour, paprika, garlic powder, onion powder, dried thyme, dried oregano, salt, and black pepper.

3. Preheat the Air Fryer to 190°C for 5 minutes.

4. Remove the chicken from the buttermilk, allowing

any excess to drip off.

5. Coat each piece of chicken in the flour mixture, pressing the coating onto the chicken to adhere.

6. Place the coated chicken pieces in the Air Fryer basket, ensuring they are not touching each other.

7. Lightly spray the chicken with vegetable oil.

8. Air fry at 190°C for 20-25 minutes or until the chicken is golden brown, crispy, and cooked through. Flip the chicken halfway through cooking for even browning.

9. While the chicken is cooking, prepare the honey mustard sauce by whisking together the mayonnaise, Dijon mustard, honey, lemon juice, salt, and black pepper in a small bowl.

10. Once cooked, remove the crispy buttermilk fried chicken from the Air Fryer and let it rest for a few minutes.

11. Serve the chicken hot with the honey mustard sauce. Enjoy this classic comfort food with a crispy and healthier twist!

Mediterranean Stuffed Eggplant Boats

Serves: 4
Prep time: 20 minutes / Cook time: 25 minutes

Ingredients:
- 2 large eggplants
- 2 tbsp olive oil
- 1 small onion, diced
- 2 cloves garlic, minced
- 1 red bell pepper, diced
- 1 yellow bell pepper, diced
- 200g cherry tomatoes, halved
- 100g crumbled feta cheese
- 50g pitted black olives, sliced
- 2 tbsp chopped fresh parsley
- 1 tbsp chopped fresh basil
- Salt and black pepper, to taste

Preparation instructions:
1. Preheat the Air Fryer to 200°C for 5 minutes.

2. Cut the eggplants in half lengthwise and scoop out the flesh, leaving about a 1cm border around the edges. Chop the scooped-out eggplant flesh and set aside.

3. Brush the inside of the eggplant boats with olive oil and place them in the Air Fryer basket, cut

side down. Air fry at 200°C for 10 minutes to soften the eggplants.

4. While the eggplants are cooking, heat the remaining olive oil in a skillet over medium heat.

5. Add the diced onion, minced garlic, and chopped eggplant flesh to the skillet. Sauté for 5 minutes or until the vegetables are softened.

6. Add the diced red bell pepper, diced yellow bell pepper, and halved cherry tomatoes to the skillet. Cook for an additional 3-4 minutes.

7. Remove the skillet from heat and stir in the crumbled feta cheese, sliced black olives, chopped parsley, and chopped basil. Season with salt and black pepper to taste. Mix well to combine.

8. Flip the eggplant boats in the Air Fryer basket so they are cut side up.

9. Spoon the Mediterranean vegetable mixture into the eggplant boats, filling them generously.

10. Air fry at 200°C for 12-15 minutes or until the eggplant boats are tender and the filling is heated through.

11. Once cooked, remove the Mediterranean stuffed eggplant boats from the Air Fryer and let them cool for a few minutes.

12. Serve the eggplant boats as a flavorful and healthy Mediterranean-inspired meal. Enjoy!

Thai Red Curry Coconut Chicken with Jasmine Rice

Serves: 4
Prep time: 15 minutes + marinating time / Cook time: 20 minutes

Ingredients:
For the Red Curry Marinade:
- 400ml coconut milk
- 2 tbsp Thai red curry paste
- 2 tbsp fish sauce
- 2 tbsp lime juice
- 2 cloves garlic, minced
- 2 tsp grated ginger
- 2 tsp brown sugar
- 500g boneless chicken breast, sliced

For the Curry and Jasmine Rice:
- 1 tbsp vegetable oil
- 1 red bell pepper, sliced
- 1 yellow bell pepper, sliced
- 1 onion, sliced
- 200g snap peas
- 200ml coconut milk
- 1 tbsp Thai red curry paste
- 2 tsp fish sauce
- 2 tsp brown sugar
- Fresh cilantro, for garnish
- Cooked jasmine rice, for serving

Preparation instructions:
1. In a bowl, whisk together the coconut milk, Thai red curry paste, fish sauce, lime juice, minced garlic, grated ginger, and brown sugar to make the red curry marinade.

2. Add the sliced chicken breast to the marinade and toss to coat. Cover and refrigerate for at least 1 hour or overnight for better flavour infusion.

3. Preheat the Air Fryer to 180°C for 5 minutes.

4. In a large skillet, heat the vegetable oil over medium heat. Add the sliced bell peppers, onion, and snap peas. Sauté for 3-4 minutes until the vegetables are slightly tender.

5. In a small bowl, mix together the coconut milk, Thai red curry paste, fish sauce, and brown sugar to make the curry sauce.

6. Add the curry sauce to the skillet with the sautéed vegetables. Stir well to combine.

7. Remove the chicken from the marinade, allowing any excess marinade to drip off. Add the chicken to the skillet with the vegetables and curry sauce.

8. Cook for 8-10 minutes or until the chicken is cooked through and the vegetables are tender.

9. While the curry is cooking, prepare the jasmine rice according to package instructions.

10. Once cooked, remove the Thai red curry coconut chicken from the skillet and let it rest for a few minutes.

11. Serve the chicken curry over cooked jasmine rice. Garnish with fresh cilantro. Enjoy this fragrant and creamy Thai-inspired dish!

Buffalo Cauliflower "Wings" with Ranch Dipping Sauce

Serves: 4
Prep time: 15 minutes / Cook time: 20 minutes

Ingredients:
For the Buffalo Cauliflower:
- 1 head cauliflower, cut into florets

- 80ml hot sauce
- 2 tbsp melted butter
- 1 tbsp apple cider vinegar
- 1 tsp garlic powder
- 1/2 tsp paprika
- Salt and black pepper, to taste

For the Ranch Dipping Sauce:
- 150ml mayonnaise
- 80 ml sour cream
- 2 tbsp chopped fresh dill
- 2 tbsp chopped fresh parsley
- 1 tbsp lemon juice
- 1 clove garlic, minced
- Salt and black pepper, to taste

Preparation instructions:
1. Preheat the Air Fryer to 200°C for 5 minutes.
2. In a bowl, whisk together the hot sauce, melted butter, apple cider vinegar, garlic powder, paprika, salt, and black pepper to make the buffalo sauce.
3. Dip each cauliflower floret into the buffalo sauce, coating it evenly. Place the coated florets in the Air Fryer basket.
4. Air fry at 200°C for 15-20 minutes or until the cauliflower is tender and crispy, flipping halfway through cooking for even browning.
5. While the cauliflower is cooking, prepare the ranch dipping sauce by combining the mayonnaise, sour cream, chopped fresh dill, chopped fresh parsley, lemon juice, minced garlic, salt, and black pepper in a small bowl. Stir well to combine.
6. Once cooked, remove the buffalo cauliflower "wings" from the Air Fryer and let them cool for a few minutes.
7. Serve the crispy buffalo cauliflower "wings" with the ranch dipping sauce. Enjoy this healthier and delicious alternative to traditional buffalo wings!

Moroccan Spiced Lamb Meatballs with Yoghurt Sauce

Serves: 4
Prep time: 20 minutes / Cook time: 20 minutes

Ingredients:
For the Lamb Meatballs:
- 500g ground lamb
- 120g breadcrumbs
- 60g chopped fresh parsley
- 2 cloves garlic, minced
- 1 small onion, grated
- 1 tsp ground cumin
- 1 tsp ground coriander
- 1/2 tsp ground cinnamon
- 1/2 tsp ground paprika
- Salt and black pepper, to taste

For the Yoghurt Sauce:
- 200g Greek yoghurt
- 2 tbsp chopped fresh mint
- 1 tbsp lemon juice
- 1 clove garlic, minced
- Salt and black pepper, to taste

Preparation instructions:
1. In a bowl, combine the ground lamb, breadcrumbs, chopped fresh parsley, minced garlic, grated onion, ground cumin, ground coriander, ground cinnamon, ground paprika, salt, and black pepper. Mix well to combine.
2. Shape the lamb mixture into small meatballs.
3. Preheat the Air Fryer to 200°C for 5 minutes.
4. Place the lamb meatballs in the Air Fryer basket, making sure they are not touching each other.
5. Air fry at 200°C for 15-20 minutes or until the meatballs are cooked through and browned, flipping them halfway through cooking for even browning.
6. While the meatballs are cooking, prepare the yoghurt sauce by combining the Greek yoghurt, chopped fresh mint, lemon juice, minced garlic, salt, and black pepper in a small bowl. Stir well to combine.
7. Once cooked, remove the Moroccan spiced lamb meatballs from the Air Fryer and let them cool for a few minutes.
8. Serve the lamb meatballs with the yoghurt sauce. Enjoy these flavorful and juicy meatballs with a refreshing yoghurt dip!

Pesto and Mozzarella Stuffed Chicken Breast with Roasted Asparagus

Serves: 4
Prep time: 15 minutes / Cook time: 25 minutes

Ingredients:
- 4 boneless, skinless chicken breasts

- 4 tbsp pesto sauce
- 4 slices mozzarella cheese
- 8-10 asparagus spears, trimmed
- 2 tbsp olive oil
- Salt and black pepper, to taste

Preparation instructions:
1. Preheat the Air Fryer to 200°C for 5 minutes.
2. Make a pocket in each chicken breast by slicing horizontally through the thickest part, being careful not to cut all the way through.
3. Spread 1 tablespoon of pesto sauce inside each chicken breast pocket. Place a slice of mozzarella cheese inside each pocket as well.
4. Season the chicken breasts with salt and black pepper.
5. Place the stuffed chicken breasts in the Air Fryer basket, making sure they are not touching each other.
6. Air fry at 200°C for 20-25 minutes or until the chicken is cooked through and the cheese is melted and bubbly.
7. While the chicken is cooking, toss the trimmed asparagus spears with olive oil, salt, and black pepper in a separate bowl.
8. Remove the chicken from the Air Fryer and set aside. Add the seasoned asparagus spears to the Air Fryer basket.
9. Air fry at 200°C for 5-7 minutes or until the asparagus is tender-crisp and slightly charred.
10. Once cooked, remove the asparagus from the Air Fryer and let it cool for a few minutes.
11. Serve the pesto and mozzarella stuffed chicken breasts with the roasted asparagus. Enjoy this delicious and elegant dish!

Balsamic Glazed Pork Tenderloin with Roasted Vegetables

Serves: 4
Prep time: 15 minutes + marinating time / Cook time: 25 minutes

Ingredients:
For the Pork Tenderloin:
- 500g pork tenderloin
- 60ml balsamic vinegar
- 2 tbsp olive oil

- 2 tbsp honey
- 2 cloves garlic, minced
- 1 tsp dried thyme
- 1/2 tsp dried rosemary
- Salt and black pepper, to taste

For the Roasted Vegetables:
- 500g mixed vegetables (such as carrots, bell peppers, zucchini, and red onion), cut into bite-sized pieces
- 2 tbsp olive oil
- 1 tsp dried oregano
- 1 tsp dried basil
- Salt and black pepper, to taste

Preparation instructions:
1. In a bowl, whisk together the balsamic vinegar, olive oil, honey, minced garlic, dried thyme, dried rosemary, salt, and black pepper to make the marinade.
2. Place the pork tenderloin in a resealable plastic bag and pour the marinade over it. Seal the bag and marinate in the refrigerator for at least 1 hour or overnight for better flavour infusion.
3. Preheat the Air Fryer to 200°C for 5 minutes.
4. Remove the pork tenderloin from the marinade, allowing any excess marinade to drip off. Reserve the marinade for later use.
5. Place the pork tenderloin in the Air Fryer basket, making sure it is not touching the sides.
6. Air fry at 200°C for 20-25 minutes or until the pork is cooked through, flipping it halfway through cooking for even browning.
7. While the pork is cooking, toss the mixed vegetables with olive oil, dried oregano, dried basil, salt, and black pepper in a separate bowl.
8. Remove the pork tenderloin from the Air Fryer and let it rest for a few minutes.
9. Add the seasoned vegetables to the Air Fryer basket.
10. Air fry at 200°C for 10-12 minutes or until the vegetables are tender and slightly caramelised, shaking the basket occasionally for even cooking.
11. While the vegetables are roasting, pour the reserved marinade into a small saucepan. Bring it to a boil over medium heat, then reduce the heat and simmer for 5 minutes or until the sauce thickens slightly.
12. Once cooked, remove the roasted vegetables from

the Air Fryer and let them cool for a few minutes.

13. Slice the pork tenderloin and drizzle it with the balsamic glaze. Serve it alongside the roasted vegetables. Enjoy this flavorful and satisfying meal!

Sesame Ginger Tofu with Stir-Fried Vegetables

Serves: 4
Prep time: 15 minutes + marinating time / Cook time: 20 minutes

Ingredients:
For the Sesame Ginger Tofu:
- 500g firm tofu, pressed and drained, cut into cubes
- 3 tbsp soy sauce
- 2 tbsp rice vinegar
- 2 tbsp honey
- 1 tbsp sesame oil
- 1 tbsp grated ginger
- 2 cloves garlic, minced
- 1 tbsp cornstarch
- 2 tbsp sesame seeds
- 2 green onions, sliced
- 2 tbsp vegetable oil, for cooking

For the Stir-Fried Vegetables:
- 2 tbsp vegetable oil
- 1 red bell pepper, sliced
- 1 yellow bell pepper, sliced
- 1 small onion, sliced
- 200g sugar snap peas
- 200g sliced mushrooms
- 2 tbsp soy sauce
- 1 tbsp oyster sauce (optional)
- Salt and black pepper, to taste

Preparation instructions:
1. In a bowl, whisk together the soy sauce, rice vinegar, honey, sesame oil, grated ginger, minced garlic, cornstarch, sesame seeds, and sliced green onions to make the marinade for the tofu.
2. Add the tofu cubes to the marinade and toss to coat. Cover and marinate in the refrigerator for at least 1 hour or overnight for better flavour infusion.
3. Preheat the Air Fryer to 200°C for 5 minutes.
4. Heat 2 tablespoons of vegetable oil in a large skillet or wok over medium-high heat. Add the

marinated tofu cubes and cook for 5-7 minutes or until the tofu is golden brown and crispy, stirring occasionally.
5. While the tofu is cooking, prepare the stir-fried vegetables. Heat 2 tablespoons of vegetable oil in a separate skillet or wok over medium-high heat. Add the sliced bell peppers, sliced onion, sugar snap peas, and sliced mushrooms. Stir-fry for 4-5 minutes or until the vegetables are crisp-tender.
6. In a small bowl, mix together the soy sauce and oyster sauce. Pour the sauce over the stir-fried vegetables and toss to coat. Season with salt and black pepper to taste.
7. Once cooked, remove the sesame ginger tofu from the skillet and let it cool for a few minutes.
8. Serve the sesame ginger tofu alongside the stir-fried vegetables. Enjoy this flavorful and protein-rich vegetarian dish!

Mexican-Style Stuffed Bell Peppers with Black Beans and Corn

Serves: 4
Prep time: 15 minutes / Cook time: 25 minutes

Ingredients:
- 4 bell peppers (assorted colours), tops removed and seeds removed
- 200g cooked rice
- 200g black beans, rinsed and drained
- 150g corn kernels
- 1 small onion, diced
- 2 cloves garlic, minced
- 1 tsp ground cumin
- 1 tsp chilli powder
- Salt and black pepper, to taste
- 200g shredded cheddar cheese
- 2 tbsp chopped fresh cilantro, for garnish
- 2 tbsp sour cream, for garnish

Preparation instructions:
1. Preheat the Air Fryer to 200°C for 5 minutes.
2. In a large skillet, heat a tablespoon of vegetable oil over medium heat. Add the diced onion and minced garlic, and sauté for 3-4 minutes until the onion is translucent.
3. Add the cooked rice, black beans, corn kernels, ground cumin, chilli powder, salt, and black pepper to the skillet. Stir well to combine and

cook for another 2-3 minutes to heat through.

4. Stuff the bell peppers with the rice and bean mixture, pressing it down gently. Place the stuffed peppers in the Air Fryer basket, making sure they are stable and not toppling over.

5. Air fry at 200°C for 20-25 minutes or until the bell peppers are tender and slightly charred, and the filling is heated through.

6. During the last 5 minutes of cooking, sprinkle shredded cheddar cheese over the stuffed bell peppers and continue air frying until the cheese is melted and bubbly.

7. Once cooked, remove the Mexican-style stuffed bell peppers from the Air Fryer and let them cool for a few minutes.

8. Garnish the stuffed bell peppers with chopped fresh cilantro and serve with a dollop of sour cream. Enjoy these flavorful and colourful Mexican-inspired stuffed peppers!

Lemon Herb Roasted Cornish Hens with Herbed Quinoa

Serves: 4
Prep time: 15 minutes + marinating time / Cook time: 35 minutes

Ingredients:
For the Lemon Herb Roasted Cornish Hens:
- 2 Cornish hens
- 2 lemons, sliced
- 4 cloves garlic, minced
- 2 tbsp chopped fresh rosemary
- 2 tbsp chopped fresh thyme
- 2 tbsp olive oil
- Salt and black pepper, to taste

For the Herbed Quinoa:
- 200g quinoa
- 400ml vegetable broth
- 2 tbsp chopped fresh parsley
- 1 tbsp chopped fresh dill
- 1 tbsp lemon juice
- Salt and black pepper, to taste

Preparation instructions:
1. In a bowl, combine the minced garlic, chopped fresh rosemary, chopped fresh thyme, olive oil, salt, and black pepper to make the marinade for the Cornish hens.

2. Place the Cornish hens in a shallow dish and rub the marinade all over them, inside and out. Place a few lemon slices inside each hen cavity. Cover and marinate in the refrigerator for at least 1 hour or overnight for better flavour infusion.

3. Preheat the Air Fryer to 180°C for 5 minutes.

4. Remove the Cornish hens from the marinade, allowing any excess marinade to drip off. Reserve the marinade for later use.

5. Place the Cornish hens in the Air Fryer basket, breast-side up. Air fry at 180°C for 30-35 minutes or until the hens are cooked through and the skin is golden brown and crispy. Check the internal temperature with a meat thermometer - it should read 74°C (165°F) in the thickest part of the meat.

6. While the Cornish hens are cooking, rinse the quinoa under cold water in a fine-mesh sieve. In a saucepan, bring the vegetable broth to a boil. Add the rinsed quinoa to the boiling broth, reduce the heat to low, cover, and simmer for 15 minutes or until the quinoa is tender and the liquid is absorbed.

7. Fluff the cooked quinoa with a fork and stir in the chopped fresh parsley, chopped fresh dill, lemon juice, salt, and black pepper.

8. Once cooked, remove the Lemon Herb Roasted Cornish hens from the Air Fryer and let them rest for a few minutes.

9. Serve the Cornish hens with a side of herbed quinoa. Enjoy this elegant and flavorful dish that's perfect for a special occasion or Sunday dinner!

Sweet and Spicy Honey Sriracha Glazed Salmon with Roasted Sweet Potatoes

Serves: 4
Prep time: 15 minutes + marinating time / Cook time: 20 minutes

Ingredients:
For the Honey Sriracha Glazed Salmon:
- 4 salmon fillets (about 150g each)
- 4 tbsp honey
- 2 tbsp soy sauce
- 2 tbsp Sriracha sauce
- 2 cloves garlic, minced

- 1 tbsp grated ginger
- 1 tbsp lime juice
- Salt and black pepper, to taste
- 2 tbsp chopped fresh cilantro, for garnish

For the Roasted Sweet Potatoes:
- 4 medium sweet potatoes, peeled and cut into wedges
- 2 tbsp olive oil
- 1 tsp paprika
- 1 tsp garlic powder
- Salt and black pepper, to taste

Preparation instructions:
1. In a bowl, whisk together the honey, soy sauce, Sriracha sauce, minced garlic, grated ginger, lime juice, salt, and black pepper to make the marinade for the salmon.
2. Place the salmon fillets in a shallow dish and pour the marinade over them, making sure they are well coated. Cover and marinate in the refrigerator for at least 30 minutes or up to 2 hours.
3. Preheat the Air Fryer to 200°C for 5 minutes.
4. In a separate bowl, toss the sweet potato wedges with olive oil, paprika, garlic powder, salt, and black pepper until evenly coated.
5. Place the marinated salmon fillets in the Air Fryer basket, skin-side down. Arrange the sweet potato wedges around the salmon, making sure they are in a single layer and not overcrowded.
6. Air fry at 200°C for 10 minutes. Open the Air Fryer, flip the salmon fillets, and give the sweet potatoes a toss for even cooking.
7. Continue air frying at 200°C for another 10 minutes or until the salmon is cooked through and the sweet potatoes are tender and slightly crispy.
8. Once cooked, remove the Sweet and Spicy Honey Sriracha Glazed Salmon and Roasted Sweet Potatoes from the Air Fryer and let them cool for a few minutes.
9. Garnish the salmon fillets with chopped fresh cilantro. Serve the salmon alongside the roasted sweet potatoes. Enjoy this delicious and healthy seafood dish!

Korean Bulgogi Beef Lettuce Wraps with Pickled Vegetables

Serves: 4
Prep time: 20 minutes + marinating time / Cook time: 10 minutes

Ingredients:
For the Bulgogi Beef:
- 500g beef sirloin, thinly sliced
- 4 tbsp soy sauce
- 2 tbsp brown sugar
- 2 tbsp sesame oil
- 2 cloves garlic, minced
- 1 tbsp grated ginger
- 1 tbsp rice vinegar
- 1 tsp sesame seeds
- 1/4 tsp black pepper
- 1/4 tsp red pepper flakes (optional)

For the Pickled Vegetables:
- 200g carrots, julienned
- 200g cucumber, julienned
- 60ml rice vinegar
- 1 tbsp sugar
- 1/2 tsp salt

For the Lettuce Wraps:
- 8-10 large lettuce leaves
- Cooked rice, for serving
- Sliced green onions, for garnish
- Toasted sesame seeds, for garnish

Preparation instructions:
1. In a bowl, combine the soy sauce, brown sugar, sesame oil, minced garlic, grated ginger, rice vinegar, sesame seeds, black pepper, and red pepper flakes (if using) to make the marinade for the Bulgogi beef.
2. Add the thinly sliced beef to the marinade and toss until all the slices are coated. Cover and marinate in the refrigerator for at least 1 hour or overnight for better flavour infusion.
3. In a separate bowl, combine the julienned carrots and cucumbers with rice vinegar, sugar, and salt to make the pickled vegetables. Mix well and let them marinate for at least 20 minutes.
4. Preheat the Air Fryer to 200°C for 5 minutes.
5. Remove the marinated beef from the refrigerator and let it come to room temperature.
6. Place the beef slices in the Air Fryer basket,

making sure they are in a single layer and not overcrowded. Air fry at 200°C for 5-6 minutes, or until the beef is cooked through and slightly caramelised.

7. While the beef is cooking, arrange the lettuce leaves on a serving platter.

8. Once the beef is cooked, transfer it to a serving bowl.

9. Serve the Korean Bulgogi beef alongside the lettuce leaves, pickled vegetables, cooked rice, sliced green onions, and toasted sesame seeds. To enjoy, take a lettuce leaf, place a spoonful of beef, pickled vegetables, and rice on it. Roll it up and enjoy these delicious and refreshing Korean lettuce wraps!

Mediterranean Grilled Vegetable Skewers with Lemon-Herb Couscous

Serves: 4
Prep time: 20 minutes + marinating time / Cook time: 10 minutes

Ingredients:
For the Grilled Vegetable Skewers:
- 200g cherry tomatoes
- 1 medium zucchini, sliced into rounds
- 1 medium yellow bell pepper, cut into chunks
- 1 medium red onion, cut into chunks
- 200g button mushrooms
- 60ml olive oil
- 2 cloves garlic, minced
- 1 tbsp lemon juice
- 1 tsp dried oregano
- 1/2 tsp dried thyme
- Salt and black pepper, to taste

For the Lemon-Herb Couscous:
- 200g couscous
- 400ml vegetable broth
- 2 tbsp chopped fresh parsley
- 2 tbsp chopped fresh mint
- 2 tbsp lemon juice
- 2 tbsp olive oil
- Salt and black pepper, to taste

Preparation instructions:
1. In a bowl, whisk together the olive oil, minced garlic, lemon juice, dried oregano, dried thyme,

salt, and black pepper to make the marinade for the grilled vegetable skewers.

2. Thread the cherry tomatoes, zucchini rounds, yellow bell pepper chunks, red onion chunks, and button mushrooms onto skewers. Place the skewers in a shallow dish and pour the marinade over them, making sure they are well coated. Cover and let them marinate for at least 30 minutes.

3. In a separate bowl, combine the couscous, vegetable broth, chopped fresh parsley, chopped fresh mint, lemon juice, olive oil, salt, and black pepper to make the lemon-herb couscous. Stir well, cover, and let it sit for about 10 minutes or until the couscous absorbs the liquid.

4. Preheat the Air Fryer to 200°C for 5 minutes.

5. Remove the vegetable skewers from the marinade, allowing any excess marinade to drip off.

6. Place the vegetable skewers in the Air Fryer basket, making sure they are in a single layer and not touching each other. Air fry at 200°C for 8-10 minutes or until the vegetables are tender and slightly charred, turning them once halfway through.

7. Once the vegetable skewers are cooked, remove them from the Air Fryer and let them cool for a few minutes.

8. Fluff the lemon-herb couscous with a fork and transfer it to a serving dish.

9. Serve the Mediterranean grilled vegetable skewers alongside the lemon-herb couscous. Enjoy the vibrant flavours of these delicious and healthy grilled vegetables with the fragrant lemon-herb couscous!

Honey Mustard Glazed Turkey Breast with Hasselback Potatoes

Serves: 4
Prep time: 20 minutes / Cook time: 30 minutes

Ingredients:
For the Turkey Breast:
- 600g turkey breast fillet
- 60ml Dijon mustard
- 60ml honey
- 2 tbsp olive oil
- 2 cloves garlic, minced
- 1 tbsp chopped fresh thyme

- Salt and black pepper, to taste

For the Hasselback Potatoes:
- 4 medium potatoes
- 2 tbsp melted butter
- 2 cloves garlic, minced
- 2 tbsp chopped fresh parsley
- Salt and black pepper, to taste

Preparation instructions:

1. Preheat the Air Fryer to 200°C for 5 minutes.
2. In a bowl, whisk together the Dijon mustard, honey, olive oil, minced garlic, chopped fresh thyme, salt, and black pepper to make the honey mustard glaze for the turkey breast.
3. Place the turkey breast fillet in a shallow dish and pour the honey mustard glaze over it, making sure it is well coated. Let it marinate for at least 15 minutes.
4. While the turkey is marinating, prepare the Hasselback potatoes. Slice the potatoes thinly, leaving the bottom intact so they stay connected. Place the potatoes in a bowl of cold water for a few minutes to remove excess starch.
5. Drain the potatoes and pat them dry with a paper towel.
6. In a separate bowl, combine the melted butter, minced garlic, chopped fresh parsley, salt, and black pepper. Brush the mixture over the potatoes, making sure to get in between the slices.
7. Place the turkey breast fillet and Hasselback potatoes in the Air Fryer basket, making sure they are in a single layer and not overcrowded.
8. Air fry at 200°C for 25-30 minutes or until the turkey is cooked through and the potatoes are golden and crispy, flipping the turkey once halfway through.
9. Once cooked, remove the honey mustard glazed turkey breast and Hasselback potatoes from the Air Fryer and let them cool for a few minutes.
10. Slice the turkey breast and serve it alongside the Hasselback potatoes. Enjoy this delightful combination of juicy turkey with a sweet and tangy glaze, paired with crispy and flavorful Hasselback potatoes!

Cajun Shrimp and Sausage Foil Packets with Corn on the Cob

Serves: 4
Prep time: 15 minutes / Cook time: 20 minutes

Ingredients:
- 400g large shrimp, peeled and deveined
- 200g smoked sausage, sliced
- 2 ears of corn, husked and cut into halves
- 1 medium red bell pepper, cut into chunks
- 1 medium green bell pepper, cut into chunks
- 1 medium red onion, cut into chunks
- 2 cloves garlic, minced
- 2 tbsp olive oil
- 1 tbsp Cajun seasoning
- 1/2 tsp smoked paprika
- 1/4 tsp cayenne pepper (optional)
- Salt and black pepper, to taste
- 2 tbsp chopped fresh parsley, for garnish
- Lemon wedges, for serving

Preparation instructions:
1. Preheat the Air Fryer to 200°C for 5 minutes.
2. In a large bowl, combine the peeled and deveined shrimp, sliced smoked sausage, corn on the cob halves, red bell pepper chunks, green bell pepper chunks, red onion chunks, minced garlic, olive oil, Cajun seasoning, smoked paprika, cayenne pepper (if using), salt, and black pepper. Toss well to coat everything evenly with the seasoning.
3. Divide the shrimp, sausage, corn, and vegetables mixture into 4 portions and place each portion on a sheet of aluminium foil. Fold the foil tightly to create a packet, ensuring it is sealed.
4. Place the foil packets in the Air Fryer basket, making sure they are not overcrowded and have some space around them for air circulation.
5. Air fry at 200°C for 18-20 minutes or until the shrimp are cooked through, the sausage is heated, and the vegetables are tender, checking for doneness after 15 minutes.
6. Once cooked, carefully remove the foil packets from the Air Fryer and let them cool for a minute or two.
7. Open the foil packets, sprinkle the Cajun shrimp and sausage mixture with chopped fresh parsley, and serve with lemon wedges on the side. These

flavorful and spicy Cajun shrimp and sausage foil packets are perfect for a quick and tasty meal!

Spicy Chipotle Lime Chicken Fajitas with Charred Peppers and Onions

Serves: 4
Prep time: 20 minutes + marinating time / Cook time: 15 minutes

Ingredients:
For the Chipotle Lime Chicken:
- 600g boneless, skinless chicken breasts, sliced into strips
- 2 tbsp olive oil
- 2 tbsp lime juice
- 2 cloves garlic, minced
- 1 tbsp chipotle pepper in adobo sauce, minced
- 1 tsp ground cumin
- 1 tsp smoked paprika
- 1/2 tsp chilli powder
- 1/2 tsp salt
- 1/4 tsp black pepper

For the Charred Peppers and Onions:
- 1 large red bell pepper, sliced
- 1 large yellow bell pepper, sliced
- 1 large green bell pepper, sliced
- 1 large red onion, sliced
- 2 tbsp olive oil
- 1/2 tsp ground cumin
- 1/2 tsp smoked paprika
- 1/2 tsp salt
- 1/4 tsp black pepper

For Serving:
- 8-10 small flour tortillas
- Sour cream, for garnish
- Chopped fresh cilantro, for garnish
- Lime wedges, for serving

Preparation instructions:
1. In a bowl, whisk together the olive oil, lime juice, minced garlic, minced chipotle pepper, ground cumin, smoked paprika, chilli powder, salt, and black pepper to make the marinade for the chipotle lime chicken.
2. Place the chicken strips in a shallow dish and pour the marinade over them, making sure they are well coated. Cover and let them marinate in the refrigerator for at least 1 hour or overnight for better flavour infusion.
3. In a separate bowl, combine the sliced red bell pepper, yellow bell pepper, green bell pepper, red onion, olive oil, ground cumin, smoked paprika, salt, and black pepper to season the charred peppers and onions.
4. Preheat the Air Fryer to 200°C for 5 minutes.
5. Remove the marinated chicken from the refrigerator and let it come to room temperature.
6. Place the chicken strips in the Air Fryer basket, making sure they are in a single layer and not overcrowded. Air fry at 200°C for 10-12 minutes or until the chicken is cooked through and slightly charred, flipping them once halfway through.
7. While the chicken is cooking, place the seasoned peppers and onions in a separate foil packet.
8. Place the foil packet in the Air Fryer basket alongside the chicken and air fry at 200°C for 8-10 minutes or until the peppers and onions are charred and tender.
9. Once cooked, remove the chicken, peppers, and onions from the Air Fryer and let them cool for a minute or two.
10. Warm the flour tortillas in the Air Fryer for a few seconds, if desired.
11. Serve the spicy chipotle lime chicken, charred peppers, and onions in warm flour tortillas. Garnish with sour cream and chopped fresh cilantro. Serve with lime wedges on the side. Enjoy these flavorful and zesty spicy chipotle lime chicken fajitas!

Air Fryer Stuffed Chicken Breast with Spinach and Feta

Serves: 4
Prep time: 15 minutes/ Cook time: 18-20 minutes

Ingredients:
- 4 boneless, skinless chicken breasts (approx. 120 g each)
- 100 g fresh spinach leaves, chopped
- 100 g crumbled feta cheese
- 1 clove garlic, minced
- 2 tbsp olive oil
- Salt and pepper, to taste
- 1 lemon, zested and juiced

- 2 tbsp all-purpose flour
- 2 tbsp Panko breadcrumbs
- 1 egg, beaten

Preparation instructions:

1. Preheat the air fryer to 200°C.
2. In a bowl, mix together the chopped spinach, feta cheese, garlic, 1 tablespoon of the olive oil, salt, pepper, and lemon zest.
3. Use a sharp knife to make a pocket in the side of each chicken breast. Spoon the spinach mixture into each pocket, and secure with toothpicks.
4. In a shallow dish, mix together the flour, salt, pepper, and lemon juice.
5. In another shallow dish, place the beaten egg.
6. In a third shallow dish, place the Panko breadcrumbs.
7. Dip each chicken breast into the flour mixture, then the egg mixture, and finally the Panko mixture, making sure it is well coated.
8. Place the chicken breasts in a single layer in the air fryer basket.
9. Brush the remaining olive oil over the chicken.
10. Cook the chicken for 18-20 minutes, turning it halfway through cooking, until the internal temperature reaches 165°F (74°C) and the chicken is crispy and golden brown.
11. Serve the chicken with a side of the honey mustard dip. Enjoy!

Mexican-Style Stuffed Chicken Breasts

For 2 Portions
Prep time: 15 minutes / Cook time: 20 minutes

Ingredients

- 2 skinless, boneless, and around 170g each chicken breasts
- 1 teaspoon chilli powder
- Smoked paprika, 1 teaspoon
- 12 teaspoon cumin powder
- Oregano, dried, 1/2 tsp.
- 1/2 teaspoon of garlic powder
- 1/8 teaspoon of onion powder
- Cayenne pepper, 1/4 tsp. (optional; taste and adjust)
- 1/8 teaspoon sea salt
- 1/8 teaspoon of ground black pepper
- 60g grated cheddar cheese
- 2 tbsp freshly chopped cilantro
- 1 tiny, seeded, and coarsely chopped jalapeño
- 1 little tomato, sliced and seeded
- 1 small avocado, diced after being peeled and pitted
- 2 teaspoon olive oil

Preparation instructions:

1. The spice mixture is made by combining the following Ingredients in a small bowl: chilli powder, smoked paprika, cumin, oregano, garlic powder, onion powder, cayenne pepper (if using), salt, and black pepper.
2. To make a pocket for stuffing, make a horizontal slit along the side of each chicken breast using a sharp knife. Take care not to cut completely through.
3. Grated cheddar cheese, cilantro, jalapeno, tomato, and avocado should be combined in a different bowl. To make the stuffing mixture, stir thoroughly.
4. Place equal amounts of the stuffing mixture in each pocket of the chicken breasts.
5. Olive oil should be used to coat the chicken breasts before being properly sprinkled with the prepared spice combination.
6. Place the packed chicken breasts in the oven and bake for 20 minutes, or until the chicken is cooked through and the internal temperature reaches 75°C.
7. The chicken breasts should be taken out and given some time to rest before serving.
8. Rice, beans, or roasted vegetables are some of your favourite side dishes to go with the Mexican-style filled chicken breasts.

Chapter 3: Fish and Seafood

Coconut Curry Cod with Mango Salsa

Serves: 4
Prep time: 15 minutes / Cook time: 12 minutes

Ingredients:

For the Coconut Curry Cod:
- 600g cod fillets
- 200ml coconut milk
- 2 tbsp curry powder
- 1 tbsp lime juice
- 1 tbsp soy sauce
- 2 cloves garlic, minced
- 1 tsp grated ginger
- 1/2 tsp turmeric powder
- 1/2 tsp cumin powder
- 1/2 tsp paprika
- Salt and black pepper, to taste

For the Mango Salsa:
- 1 ripe mango, diced
- 1/2 red onion, finely chopped
- 1/2 red bell pepper, diced
- 1/2 green bell pepper, diced
- 2 tbsp chopped fresh cilantro
- 1 tbsp lime juice
- 1 tbsp olive oil
- Salt, to taste

Preparation instructions:

1. Preheat the Air Fryer to 200°C for 5 minutes.
2. In a bowl, combine the coconut milk, curry powder, lime juice, soy sauce, minced garlic, grated ginger, turmeric powder, cumin powder, paprika, salt, and black pepper. Stir well to make the coconut curry marinade.
3. Pat dry the cod fillets using paper towels. Place the cod fillets in a shallow dish and pour the coconut curry marinade over them, ensuring the fillets are coated evenly. Let them marinate for 10 minutes.
4. While the cod is marinating, prepare the mango salsa. In a separate bowl, combine the diced mango, finely chopped red onion, diced red bell pepper, diced green bell pepper, chopped fresh cilantro, lime juice, olive oil, and salt. Toss well to mix all the Ingredients. Set aside.
5. Place the marinated cod fillets in the Air Fryer basket, ensuring they are not overcrowded. Air fry at 200°C for 10-12 minutes or until the cod is cooked through and flakes easily with a fork.
6. Once cooked, remove the cod from the Air Fryer and let it rest for a minute.
7. Serve the coconut curry cod with a generous scoop of mango salsa on top. Enjoy this delightful and flavorful coconut curry cod with vibrant mango salsa!

Lemon Dill Salmon Cakes with Caper Remoulade

Serves: 4
Prep time: 15 minutes / Cook time: 12 minutes

Ingredients:
- For the Salmon Cakes:
- 400g cooked salmon, flaked
- 60g breadcrumbs
- 2 tbsp chopped fresh dill
- 2 tbsp mayonnaise
- 1 tbsp Dijon mustard
- 1 tbsp lemon juice
- 1 tsp lemon zest
- 1/2 tsp garlic powder
- 1/4 tsp salt
- 1/4 tsp black pepper
- 1 large egg, beaten
- 2 tbsp olive oil, for frying
- For the Caper Remoulade:
- 100ml mayonnaise
- 2 tbsp capers, chopped
- 1 tbsp lemon juice
- 1 tbsp chopped fresh parsley
- 1 tsp Dijon mustard
- 1/4 tsp paprika
- Salt and black pepper, to taste

Preparation instructions:

1. In a bowl, combine the flaked cooked salmon, breadcrumbs, chopped fresh dill, mayonnaise, Dijon mustard, lemon juice, lemon zest, garlic

powder, salt, black pepper, and beaten egg. Mix well until all the Ingredients are combined and the mixture holds together.

2. Shape the salmon mixture into patties, about 8-10 patties depending on the desired size.

3. Preheat the Air Fryer to 180°C for 5 minutes.

4. Brush the salmon cakes with olive oil on both sides.

5. Place the salmon cakes in the Air Fryer basket, ensuring they are not overcrowded. Air fry at 180°C for 10-12 minutes, flipping them once halfway through, or until they are golden brown and crispy.

6. While the salmon cakes are cooking, prepare the caper remoulade. In a bowl, combine the mayonnaise, chopped capers, lemon juice, chopped fresh parsley, Dijon mustard, paprika, salt, and black pepper. Stir well to combine all the Ingredients.

7. Once the salmon cakes are cooked, remove them from the Air Fryer and let them cool for a minute.

8. Serve the lemon dill salmon cakes with a dollop of caper remoulade on top. Enjoy these delicious and zesty salmon cakes with tangy caper remoulade!

9. Note: The cooking time may vary depending on the thickness and size of the salmon cakes. Adjust the cooking time accordingly.

Spicy Tandoori Grilled Fish Tacos with Mint Chutney

Serves: 4
Prep time: 15 minutes / Cook time: 10 minutes

Ingredients:

For the Spicy Tandoori Grilled Fish:
- 600g white fish fillets (such as cod or tilapia)
- 100g plain yoghurt
- 2 tbsp tandoori masala
- 1 tbsp lemon juice
- 1 tbsp olive oil
- 1/2 tsp ground cumin
- 1/2 tsp ground coriander
- 1/4 tsp turmeric powder
- 1/4 tsp cayenne pepper (adjust to taste)
- 1/4 tsp salt

For the Mint Chutney:
- 200g fresh mint leaves

- 120g fresh cilantro leaves
- 1 green chilli, chopped
- 2 tbsp lemon juice
- 1 tbsp chopped red onion
- 1 tbsp plain yoghurt
- 1/2 tsp sugar
- 1/4 tsp salt

For the Tacos:
- 8 small corn or flour tortillas
- Shredded lettuce
- Sliced red onion
- Chopped fresh cilantro
- Lime wedges, for serving

Preparation instructions:

1. Preheat the Air Fryer to 200°C for 5 minutes.

2. In a bowl, combine the plain yoghurt, tandoori masala, lemon juice, olive oil, ground cumin, ground coriander, turmeric powder, cayenne pepper, and salt. Mix well to make the tandoori marinade.

3. Pat dry the fish fillets using paper towels. Place the fish fillets in a shallow dish and pour the tandoori marinade over them, ensuring the fillets are coated evenly. Let them marinate for 10 minutes.

4. While the fish is marinating, prepare the mint chutney. In a blender or food processor, combine the fresh mint leaves, fresh cilantro leaves, green chilli, lemon juice, chopped red onion, plain yoghurt, sugar, and salt. Blend until smooth and well combined. Set aside.

5. Place the marinated fish fillets in the Air Fryer basket, ensuring they are not overcrowded. Air fry at 200°C for 8-10 minutes or until the fish is cooked through and flakes easily with a fork.

6. Once cooked, remove the fish from the Air Fryer and let it rest for a minute.

7. Warm the tortillas in the Air Fryer for a few seconds, if desired.

8. To assemble the tacos, place a spoonful of mint chutney on each tortilla. Add a few pieces of grilled fish on top. Garnish with shredded lettuce, sliced red onion, chopped fresh cilantro, and a squeeze of lime juice.

9. Serve the spicy tandoori grilled fish tacos with additional mint chutney on the side. Enjoy these flavorful and spicy fish tacos with refreshing mint

chutney!

10.Note: Adjust the amount of cayenne pepper in the marinade to suit your spice preference.

Teriyaki Glazed Mahi-Mahi with Pineapple Salsa

Serves: 4
Prep time: 15 minutes / Cook time: 10 minutes

Ingredients:
For the Teriyaki Glazed Mahi-Mahi:
- 600g mahi-mahi fillets
- 4 tbsp teriyaki sauce
- 2 tbsp honey
- 1 tbsp soy sauce
- 1 tbsp rice vinegar
- 1 tbsp grated ginger
- 2 cloves garlic, minced
- 1/4 tsp black pepper

For the Pineapple Salsa:
- 240g diced fresh pineapple
- 60g diced red bell pepper
- 60g diced yellow bell pepper
- 60g diced red onion
- 2 tbsp chopped fresh cilantro
- 1 tbsp lime juice
- 1/2 tsp honey
- 1/4 tsp salt

Preparation instructions:
1. Preheat the Air Fryer to 200°C for 5 minutes.
2. In a bowl, whisk together the teriyaki sauce, honey, soy sauce, rice vinegar, grated ginger, minced garlic, and black pepper to make the teriyaki glaze.
3. Pat dry the mahi-mahi fillets using paper towels. Brush both sides of the fillets with the teriyaki glaze.
4. In another bowl, combine the diced fresh pineapple, diced red bell pepper, diced yellow bell pepper, diced red onion, chopped fresh cilantro, lime juice, honey, and salt to make the pineapple salsa. Mix well to combine all the Ingredients.
5. Place the marinated mahi-mahi fillets in the Air Fryer basket, ensuring they are not overcrowded. Air fry at 200°C for 8-10 minutes or until the fish is cooked through and flakes easily with a fork.
6. Once cooked, remove the mahi-mahi from the Air

Fryer and let it rest for a minute.

7. Serve the teriyaki glazed mahi-mahi with a generous scoop of pineapple salsa on top. Enjoy this delicious and tangy teriyaki glazed fish with the vibrant flavours of pineapple salsa!
8. Note: Adjust the cooking time depending on the thickness of the mahi-mahi fillets. Thicker fillets may require additional cooking time.

Mediterranean Herb Crusted Sea Bass with Roasted Tomatoes

Serves: 4
Prep time: 15 minutes / Cook time: 10 minutes

Ingredients:
For the Herb Crust:
- 80g breadcrumbs
- 2 tbsp chopped fresh parsley
- 1 tbsp chopped fresh dill
- 1 tbsp chopped fresh basil
- 1 tbsp chopped fresh oregano
- 1 tbsp grated lemon zest
- 2 cloves garlic, minced
- 2 tbsp olive oil
- Salt and black pepper, to taste

For the Sea Bass:
- 600g sea bass fillets
- 2 tbsp olive oil
- Salt and black pepper, to taste

For the Roasted Tomatoes:
- 400g cherry tomatoes
- 2 tbsp olive oil
- 1 tsp dried thyme
- Salt and black pepper, to taste

Preparation instructions:
1. Preheat the Air Fryer to 200°C for 5 minutes.
2. In a bowl, combine the breadcrumbs, chopped fresh parsley, chopped fresh dill, chopped fresh basil, chopped fresh oregano, grated lemon zest, minced garlic, olive oil, salt, and black pepper. Mix well to make the herb crust.
3. Pat dry the sea bass fillets using paper towels. Rub both sides of the fillets with olive oil and season with salt and black pepper.
4. Press the herb crust mixture onto the top side of each sea bass fillet, ensuring an even coating.

5. In another bowl, toss the cherry tomatoes with olive oil, dried thyme, salt, and black pepper to make the roasted tomatoes.

6. Place the herb-crusted sea bass fillets and the roasted tomatoes in the Air Fryer basket, ensuring they are not overcrowded. Air fry at 200°C for 8-10 minutes or until the sea bass is cooked through and flakes easily with a fork, and the tomatoes are roasted and slightly softened.

7. Once cooked, remove the sea bass and roasted tomatoes from the Air Fryer and let them rest for a minute.

8. Serve the Mediterranean herb-crusted sea bass with a side of roasted tomatoes. Enjoy this flavorful and aromatic sea bass dish with the burst of roasted tomatoes!

9. Note: Adjust the cooking time depending on the thickness of the sea bass fillets. Thicker fillets may require additional cooking time.

Blackened Scallops with Avocado Lime Crema

Serves: 4
Prep time: 15 minutes / Cook time: 6 minutes

Ingredients:
For the Blackened Seasoning:
- 2 tsp paprika
- 1 tsp dried thyme
- 1 tsp dried oregano
- 1 tsp garlic powder
- 1 tsp onion powder
- 1/2 tsp cayenne pepper (adjust to taste)
- 1/2 tsp salt
- 1/4 tsp black pepper

For the Scallops:
- 16 large scallops
- 2 tbsp olive oil

For the Avocado Lime Crema:
- 1 ripe avocado
- 120ml plain yoghurt
- 2 tbsp lime juice
- 1 tbsp chopped fresh cilantro
- 1/2 tsp garlic powder
- 1/4 tsp salt
- 1/4 tsp black pepper

Preparation instructions:
1. Preheat the Air Fryer to 200°C for 5 minutes.
2. In a small bowl, combine the paprika, dried thyme, dried oregano, garlic powder, onion powder, cayenne pepper, salt, and black pepper to make the blackened seasoning.
3. Pat dry the scallops using paper towels. Brush both sides of the scallops with olive oil.
4. Sprinkle the blackened seasoning generously on both sides of the scallops, pressing gently to adhere the seasoning to the scallops.
5. In a blender or food processor, combine the ripe avocado, plain yoghurt, lime juice, chopped fresh cilantro, garlic powder, salt, and black pepper to make the avocado lime crema. Blend until smooth and well combined.
6. Place the seasoned scallops in the Air Fryer basket, ensuring they are not overcrowded. Air fry at 200°C for 6 minutes or until the scallops are cooked through and slightly opaque in the centre.
7. Once cooked, remove the scallops from the Air Fryer and let them rest for a minute.
8. Serve the blackened scallops with a drizzle of avocado lime crema on top. Enjoy these perfectly seasoned scallops with creamy avocado lime crema!
9. Note: Adjust the cooking time depending on the size and thickness of the scallops. Cook until they are cooked through and reach an internal temperature of 54°C (130°F).

Harissa Spiced Grilled Shrimp Skewers with Tzatziki Sauce

Serves: 4
Prep time: 15 minutes / Cook time: 6 minutes

Ingredients:
For the Harissa Spiced Shrimp:
- 600g large shrimp, peeled and deveined
- 2 tbsp olive oil
- 2 tbsp harissa paste
- 1 tbsp lemon juice
- 2 cloves garlic, minced
- 1/2 tsp ground cumin
- 1/2 tsp ground coriander
- 1/4 tsp smoked paprika
- 1/4 tsp salt
- 1/4 tsp black pepper

For the Tzatziki Sauce:
- 200g Greek yoghurt
- 1/2 cucumber, grated and squeezed to remove excess moisture
- 1 clove garlic, minced
- 1 tbsp chopped fresh dill
- 1 tbsp lemon juice
- 1 tbsp olive oil
- Salt and black pepper, to taste

For the Skewers:
- 8 wooden or metal skewers

Preparation instructions:

1. Preheat the Air Fryer to 200°C for 5 minutes.
2. In a bowl, combine the olive oil, harissa paste, lemon juice, minced garlic, ground cumin, ground coriander, smoked paprika, salt, and black pepper to make the harissa marinade.
3. Pat dry the shrimp using paper towels. Place the shrimp in a shallow dish and pour the harissa marinade over them, ensuring they are coated evenly. Let them marinate for 10 minutes.
4. If using wooden skewers, soak them in water for 15 minutes to prevent burning.
5. In the meantime, prepare the tzatziki sauce. In a bowl, combine the Greek yoghurt, grated cucumber, minced garlic, chopped fresh dill, lemon juice, olive oil, salt, and black pepper. Mix well to make the tzatziki sauce.
6. Thread the marinated shrimp onto skewers, evenly distributing them.
7. Place the shrimp skewers in the Air Fryer basket, ensuring they are not overcrowded. Air fry at 200°C for 6 minutes or until the shrimp are pink, opaque, and cooked through.
8. Once cooked, remove the shrimp skewers from the Air Fryer and let them rest for a minute.
9. Serve the harissa spiced shrimp skewers with a side of tzatziki sauce. Enjoy these spicy and flavorful shrimp skewers with cool and creamy tzatziki sauce!
10. Note: Adjust the cooking time depending on the size of the shrimp. Cook until they are pink, opaque, and cooked through.

Pesto Parmesan Crusted Halibut with Roasted Vegetables

Serves: 4
Prep time: 15 minutes / Cook time: 12 minutes

Ingredients:
For the Pesto Parmesan Crust:
- 60g grated Parmesan cheese
- 40g breadcrumbs
- 2 tbsp prepared pesto
- 2 tbsp chopped fresh parsley
- 1 tbsp lemon juice
- 1 tbsp olive oil

For the Halibut:
- 600g halibut fillets
- Salt and black pepper, to taste
- For the Roasted Vegetables:
- 400g mixed vegetables (such as bell peppers, zucchini, and cherry tomatoes), cut into bite-sized pieces
- 2 tbsp olive oil
- 1 tsp dried Italian seasoning
- Salt and black pepper, to taste

Preparation instructions:
1. Preheat the Air Fryer to 200°C for 5 minutes.
2. In a bowl, combine the grated Parmesan cheese, breadcrumbs, prepared pesto, chopped fresh parsley, lemon juice, and olive oil to make the pesto Parmesan crust.
3. Pat dry the halibut fillets using paper towels. Season both sides of the fillets with salt and black pepper.
4. Press the pesto Parmesan crust mixture onto the top side of each halibut fillet, ensuring an even coating.
5. In another bowl, toss the mixed vegetables with olive oil, dried Italian seasoning, salt, and black pepper to make the roasted vegetables.
6. Place the pesto Parmesan-crusted halibut fillets and the seasoned vegetables in the Air Fryer basket, ensuring they are not overcrowded. Air fry at 200°C for 12 minutes or until the halibut is cooked through and flakes easily with a fork, and the vegetables are roasted and tender.
7. Once cooked, remove the halibut and roasted

vegetables from the Air Fryer and let them rest for a minute.

8. Serve the pesto Parmesan-crusted halibut with a side of roasted vegetables. Enjoy this delightful combination of flavorful halibut with roasted vegetables!

9. Note: Adjust the cooking time depending on the thickness of the halibut fillets. Thicker fillets may require additional cooking time.

Thai Red Curry Mussels with Coconut Rice

Serves: 4
Prep time: 15 minutes / Cook time: 8 minutes

Ingredients:
For the Thai Red Curry Sauce:
- 2 tbsp red curry paste
- 400ml coconut milk
- 2 tbsp fish sauce
- 1 tbsp lime juice
- 1 tbsp brown sugar
- 1 stalk lemongrass, smashed
- 4 kaffir lime leaves
- 1/2 tsp grated ginger
- For the Mussels:
- 1kg fresh mussels, cleaned and debearded
- 2 cloves garlic, minced
- 1 red chilli, sliced
- 60g chopped fresh cilantro

For the Coconut Rice:
- 300g jasmine rice
- 400ml coconut milk
- 400ml water
- 1/2 tsp salt

Preparation instructions:
1. Preheat the Air Fryer to 200°C for 5 minutes.
2. In a bowl, whisk together the red curry paste, coconut milk, fish sauce, lime juice, brown sugar, grated ginger, smashed lemongrass, and kaffir lime leaves to make the Thai red curry sauce.
3. In a separate bowl, combine the cleaned and debearded mussels with minced garlic, sliced red chilli, and chopped fresh cilantro.
4. In a saucepan, combine the jasmine rice, coconut milk, water, and salt for the coconut rice. Bring to a boil, then reduce the heat to low, cover, and

simmer for 15 minutes or until the rice is cooked and the liquid is absorbed.

5. Place the mussels mixture in the Air Fryer basket, ensuring they are spread evenly. Pour the Thai red curry sauce over the mussels.
6. Air fry at 200°C for 8 minutes or until the mussels have opened and are cooked through.
7. Once cooked, remove the mussels from the Air Fryer and discard any unopened mussels.
8. Serve the Thai red curry mussels over a bed of coconut rice. Enjoy this aromatic and flavorful dish with a taste of Thailand!
9. Note: Discard any mussels that do not open after cooking.

Chimichurri Grilled Swordfish with Grilled Corn Salad

Serves: 4
Prep time: 15 minutes / Cook time: 10 minutes

Ingredients:
For the Chimichurri Sauce:
- 200g fresh parsley leaves
- 120g fresh cilantro leaves
- 3 cloves garlic
- 2 tbsp red wine vinegar
- 2 tbsp lime juice
- 1/2 tsp dried oregano
- 1/2 tsp red pepper flakes
- 1/4 tsp salt
- 1/4 tsp black pepper
- 120ml olive oil

For the Grilled Swordfish:
- 600g swordfish steaks
- 2 tbsp olive oil
- Salt and black pepper, to taste

For the Grilled Corn Salad:
- 4 ears of corn, husked
- 2 tbsp olive oil
- 1 red bell pepper, diced
- 1 green bell pepper, diced
- 1/2 red onion, diced
- 2 tbsp chopped fresh cilantro
- 1 tbsp lime juice
- Salt and black pepper, to taste

Preparation instructions:
1. Preheat the Air Fryer to 200°C for 5 minutes.

2. In a blender or food processor, combine the fresh parsley leaves, fresh cilantro leaves, garlic, red wine vinegar, lime juice, dried oregano, red pepper flakes, salt, black pepper, and olive oil to make the chimichurri sauce. Blend until smooth and well combined.

3. Pat dry the swordfish steaks using paper towels. Brush both sides of the swordfish steaks with olive oil. Season with salt and black pepper.

4. Place the swordfish steaks in the Air Fryer basket, ensuring they are not overcrowded. Air fry at 200°C for 10 minutes or until the swordfish is cooked through and flakes easily with a fork.

5. While the swordfish is cooking, brush the ears of corn with olive oil. Place them in the Air Fryer basket and air fry at 200°C for 5 minutes or until the corn is lightly charred. Remove the corn from the Air Fryer and let it cool slightly.

6. Cut the grilled corn kernels off the cob and place them in a bowl. Add diced red bell pepper, diced green bell pepper, diced red onion, chopped fresh cilantro, lime juice, salt, and black pepper. Toss to combine, creating the grilled corn salad.

7. Once cooked, remove the swordfish steaks from the Air Fryer and let them rest for a minute.

8. Serve the chimichurri grilled swordfish with a side of grilled corn salad. Enjoy this vibrant and flavorful dish with the perfect balance of tangy chimichurri sauce and fresh grilled corn salad!

9. Note: Adjust the cooking time depending on the thickness of the swordfish steaks. Thicker steaks may require additional cooking time.

Baja Fish Tacos with Chipotle Lime Crema and Pickled Onions

Serves: 4
Prep time: 20 minutes / Cook time: 10 minutes

Ingredients:
For the Baja Fish:
- 600g white fish fillets (such as cod or haddock), cut into strips
- 120g all-purpose flour
- 1 tsp chilli powder
- 1/2 tsp paprika
- 1/2 tsp garlic powder
- 1/2 tsp salt
- 1/4 tsp black pepper
- 120ml beer (such as lager)

For the Chipotle Lime Crema:
- 120ml sour cream
- 1 tbsp lime juice
- 1 tsp chipotle pepper in adobo sauce, minced
- 1/4 tsp salt
- 1/4 tsp black pepper

For the Pickled Onions:
- 1 red onion, thinly sliced
- 60ml white vinegar
- 60ml water
- 1 tbsp sugar
- 1/2 tsp salt

For Serving:
- 8 small flour tortillas
- Shredded lettuce
- Chopped fresh cilantro
- Lime wedges

Preparation instructions:
1. Preheat the Air Fryer to 200°C for 5 minutes.
2. In a shallow dish, combine the all-purpose flour, chilli powder, paprika, garlic powder, salt, and black pepper for the Baja fish coating. Mix well.
3. Dip each fish strip into the beer, allowing the excess to drip off. Then coat the fish in the seasoned flour mixture, pressing gently to adhere the coating to the fish.
4. Place the coated fish strips in the Air Fryer basket, ensuring they are not overcrowded. Air fry at 200°C for 8-10 minutes or until the fish is golden brown and cooked through.
5. While the fish is cooking, prepare the chipotle lime crema. In a bowl, combine the sour cream, lime juice, minced chipotle pepper, salt, and black pepper. Mix well to make the chipotle lime crema.
6. In another bowl, combine the thinly sliced red onion, white vinegar, water, sugar, and salt for the pickled onions. Let the onions sit in the mixture for at least 10 minutes, stirring occasionally.
7. Once cooked, remove the fish strips from the Air Fryer and let them rest for a minute.
8. Warm the flour tortillas in the Air Fryer for a few seconds, if desired.
9. To assemble the tacos, spread a dollop of chipotle

lime crema on each tortilla. Top with shredded lettuce, cooked Baja fish strips, pickled onions, and chopped fresh cilantro. Squeeze lime juice over the fillings.

10. Serve the Baja fish tacos immediately. Enjoy these delicious and zesty fish tacos with a delightful combination of flavours and textures!

Szechuan Style Spicy Garlic Shrimp with Stir-Fried Vegetables

Serves: 4
Prep time: 15 minutes / Cook time: 10 minutes

Ingredients:

For the Spicy Garlic Shrimp:
- 400g large shrimp, peeled and deveined
- 2 tbsp soy sauce
- 1 tbsp rice vinegar
- 1 tbsp honey
- 2 tsp Szechuan peppercorns, crushed
- 3 cloves garlic, minced
- 1 tsp grated ginger
- 1/2 tsp chilli flakes (adjust to taste)
- 2 tbsp vegetable oil

For the Stir-Fried Vegetables:
- 200g broccoli florets
- 1 red bell pepper, sliced
- 1 yellow bell pepper, sliced
- 1 carrot, julienned
- 1 small onion, thinly sliced
- 2 cloves garlic, minced
- 2 tbsp soy sauce
- 1 tbsp oyster sauce
- 1 tbsp sesame oil
- Salt and black pepper, to taste

Preparation instructions:

1. Preheat the Air Fryer to 200°C for 5 minutes.
2. In a bowl, combine the soy sauce, rice vinegar, honey, crushed Szechuan peppercorns, minced garlic, grated ginger, and chilli flakes. Mix well to make the marinade for the shrimp.
3. Add the peeled and deveined shrimp to the marinade and toss to coat evenly. Let the shrimp marinate for 10 minutes.
4. In the meantime, prepare the stir-fried vegetables. In a bowl, combine the soy sauce, oyster sauce,

and sesame oil. Set aside.

5. Heat 1 tablespoon of vegetable oil in a wok or large skillet over high heat. Add the broccoli florets, sliced red bell pepper, sliced yellow bell pepper, julienned carrot, and thinly sliced onion. Stir-fry for 3-4 minutes or until the vegetables are crisp-tender. Add the minced garlic and stir-fry for an additional 1 minute.
6. Pour the sauce mixture over the stir-fried vegetables. Stir well to coat the vegetables in the sauce. Season with salt and black pepper to taste. Continue to stir-fry for another 1-2 minutes. Remove the stir-fried vegetables from the heat and set aside.
7. Brush the Air Fryer basket with the remaining 1 tablespoon of vegetable oil. Place the marinated shrimp in the Air Fryer basket, ensuring they are not overcrowded. Air fry at 200°C for 5-6 minutes or until the shrimp are cooked through and slightly crispy.
8. Serve the spicy garlic shrimp alongside the stir-fried vegetables. Enjoy this Szechuan-style dish with a kick of spice and deliciously stir-fried vegetables!

Mediterranean Stuffed Squid with Lemon and Feta

Serves: 4
Prep time: 20 minutes / Cook time: 15 minutes

Ingredients:
- 8 medium squid tubes
- 200g cooked white rice
- 100g feta cheese, crumbled
- 50g Kalamata olives, pitted and chopped
- 1 small tomato, diced
- 2 tbsp chopped fresh parsley
- 1 tbsp chopped fresh dill
- 2 tbsp lemon juice
- 2 tbsp olive oil
- Salt and black pepper, to taste

Preparation instructions:

1. Preheat the Air Fryer to 200°C for 5 minutes.
2. In a bowl, combine the cooked white rice, crumbled feta cheese, chopped Kalamata olives, diced tomato, chopped fresh parsley, chopped fresh dill, lemon juice, olive oil, salt, and black

pepper. Mix well to make the stuffing for the squid.

3. Stuff each squid tube with the prepared rice and feta stuffing, leaving some space at the end to secure with a toothpick.

4. Brush the Air Fryer basket with olive oil. Place the stuffed squid tubes in the Air Fryer basket, ensuring they are not overcrowded. Air fry at 200°C for 12-15 minutes or until the squid is cooked and tender, and the filling is heated through.

5. Once cooked, remove the stuffed squid from the Air Fryer and let cool for a few minutes. Remove the toothpicks before serving.

6. Serve the Mediterranean stuffed squid with lemon wedges on the side. Enjoy the combination of flavours from the savoury stuffing and the tender squid!

Garlic Butter Grilled Clams with Fresh Herbs

Serves: 4
Prep time: 10 minutes / Cook time: 8 minutes

Ingredients:
- 500g fresh clams
- 3 cloves garlic, minced
- 2 tbsp unsalted butter, melted
- 2 tbsp chopped fresh parsley
- 1 tbsp chopped fresh thyme
- 1 tbsp chopped fresh chives
- 1 tbsp lemon juice
- Salt and black pepper, to taste

Preparation instructions:
1. Preheat the Air Fryer to 200°C for 5 minutes.
2. Rinse the fresh clams under cold water and scrub off any dirt or debris. Discard any clams that are open or cracked.
3. In a bowl, combine the minced garlic, melted butter, chopped fresh parsley, chopped fresh thyme, chopped fresh chives, lemon juice, salt, and black pepper. Mix well to make the garlic herb butter.
4. Brush the Air Fryer basket with olive oil. Place the fresh clams in the Air Fryer basket, ensuring they are not overcrowded. Drizzle the garlic herb butter over the clams.

5. Air fry at 200°C for 6-8 minutes or until the clams open and are cooked through. Discard any clams that do not open.

6. Once cooked, remove the garlic butter grilled clams from the Air Fryer and transfer to a serving dish. Pour any remaining garlic herb butter from the Air Fryer over the clams.

7. Serve the garlic butter grilled clams with fresh lemon wedges on the side. Enjoy these succulent and flavorful clams as an appetiser or part of a seafood feast!

Pecan Crusted Red Snapper with Maple Dijon Glaze

Serves: 4
Prep time: 15 minutes / Cook time: 12 minutes

Ingredients:
- 4 red snapper fillets
- 100g pecans, finely chopped
- 50g breadcrumbs
- 2 tbsp Dijon mustard
- 2 tbsp maple syrup
- 1 tbsp olive oil
- 1 tsp paprika
- 1/2 tsp garlic powder
- Salt and black pepper, to taste

Preparation instructions:
1. Preheat the Air Fryer to 200°C for 5 minutes.
2. In a shallow bowl, combine the finely chopped pecans, breadcrumbs, paprika, garlic powder, salt, and black pepper. Mix well.
3. In a separate bowl, whisk together the Dijon mustard, maple syrup, and olive oil.
4. Brush the red snapper fillets with the maple Dijon glaze on both sides. Coat the fillets evenly with the pecan and breadcrumb mixture, pressing gently to adhere.
5. Brush the Air Fryer basket with olive oil. Place the coated red snapper fillets in the Air Fryer basket, ensuring they are not overlapping.
6. Air fry at 200°C for 10-12 minutes or until the pecan crust is golden and the fish is cooked through and flakes easily with a fork.
7. Once cooked, remove the pecan crusted red snapper from the Air Fryer and let rest for a few minutes before serving.

8. Serve the pecan crusted red snapper with a side of lemon wedges and your favourite vegetables or salad. Enjoy the delightful combination of crunchy pecan crust and sweet-savoury glaze on tender red snapper!

Sesame Crusted Tuna Steaks with Wasabi Mayo

Serves: 4
Prep time: 10 minutes / Cook time: 8 minutes

Ingredients:
- 4 tuna steaks
- 50g sesame seeds
- 2 tbsp soy sauce
- 1 tbsp sesame oil
- 1 tbsp lime juice
- 1 tsp grated ginger
- 1/2 tsp garlic powder
- Salt and black pepper, to taste
- For the Wasabi Mayo:
- 4 tbsp mayonnaise
- 1 tsp wasabi paste (adjust to taste)

Preparation instructions:
1. Preheat the Air Fryer to 200°C for 5 minutes.
2. In a shallow bowl, spread the sesame seeds. Season the tuna steaks with salt and black pepper on both sides.
3. In a separate bowl, whisk together the soy sauce, sesame oil, lime juice, grated ginger, and garlic powder. This will be used as a marinade for the tuna steaks.
4. Dip each tuna steak into the marinade, coating both sides. Then press each side of the tuna steak into the sesame seeds, ensuring they adhere well.
5. Brush the Air Fryer basket with olive oil. Place the sesame-crusted tuna steaks in the Air Fryer basket, ensuring they are not overlapping.
6. Air fry at 200°C for 6-8 minutes for medium-rare doneness or adjust the cooking time to your preferred level of doneness.
7. While the tuna steaks are cooking, prepare the wasabi mayo by combining the mayonnaise and wasabi paste in a small bowl. Adjust the amount of wasabi paste to your desired level of spiciness.
8. Once cooked, remove the sesame crusted tuna steaks from the Air Fryer and let rest for a few

minutes before slicing.
9. Serve the sesame crusted tuna steaks with a dollop of wasabi mayo on top. Pair with steamed rice or a fresh salad for a delicious and satisfying meal!

Spicy Mango Glazed Salmon with Quinoa Pilaf

Serves: 4
Prep time: 15 minutes / Cook time: 15 minutes

Ingredients:
For the Spicy Mango Glaze:
- 1 ripe mango, peeled and pitted
- 2 tbsp lime juice
- 2 tbsp honey
- 1 tbsp soy sauce
- 1 tbsp sriracha sauce (adjust to taste)

For the Salmon:
- 4 salmon fillets
- 2 tbsp olive oil
- 1 tsp smoked paprika
- 1/2 tsp garlic powder
- Salt and black pepper, to taste

For the Quinoa Pilaf:
- 200g quinoa
- 400ml vegetable broth
- 1 small onion, finely chopped
- 1 small red bell pepper, diced
- 1 small yellow bell pepper, diced
- 1 small zucchini, diced
- 2 cloves garlic, minced
- 2 tbsp olive oil
- 1 tsp ground cumin
- 1/2 tsp ground coriander
- Salt and black pepper, to taste
- 2 tbsp chopped fresh cilantro (coriander) for garnish

Preparation instructions:
1. Preheat the Air Fryer to 200°C for 5 minutes.
2. In a blender or food processor, blend the ripe mango, lime juice, honey, soy sauce, and sriracha sauce until smooth. This will be the spicy mango glaze.
3. Brush the salmon fillets with olive oil on both sides. Season with smoked paprika, garlic powder, salt, and black pepper.
4. Brush the Air Fryer basket with olive oil. Place

the seasoned salmon fillets in the Air Fryer basket, ensuring they are not overlapping.

5. Air fry at 200°C for 10-12 minutes or until the salmon is cooked to your preferred level of doneness and the glaze is slightly caramelised.

6. While the salmon is cooking, rinse the quinoa under cold water and drain well.

7. In a saucepan, heat 1 tablespoon of olive oil over medium heat. Add the finely chopped onion and sauté until translucent. Add the minced garlic, diced red and yellow bell peppers, and diced zucchini. Sauté for another 3-4 minutes or until the vegetables are tender.

8. Add the rinsed quinoa to the saucepan and stir to coat the grains with the vegetable mixture. Add the vegetable broth, ground cumin, ground coriander, salt, and black pepper. Bring to a boil, then reduce the heat to low, cover, and simmer for about 15 minutes or until the quinoa is cooked and the liquid is absorbed.

9. Fluff the quinoa with a fork and stir in the chopped fresh cilantro.

10. Serve the spicy mango glazed salmon over a bed of quinoa pilaf. Drizzle any remaining glaze over the salmon and garnish with additional cilantro, if desired. Enjoy the sweet and spicy flavours of the mango glaze paired with the nutty quinoa pilaf!

Grilled Octopus Salad with Citrus Vinaigrette

Serves: 4
Prep time: 20 minutes / Cook time: 15 minutes

Ingredients:
For the Grilled Octopus:
- 800g octopus tentacles
- 2 tbsp olive oil
- 2 cloves garlic, minced
- 1 tbsp chopped fresh parsley
- 1 tsp dried oregano
- Salt and black pepper, to taste
For the Citrus Vinaigrette:
- 2 tbsp lemon juice
- 2 tbsp orange juice
- 2 tbsp lime juice
- 2 tbsp extra-virgin olive oil
- 1 tbsp honey
- 1 clove garlic, minced
- Salt and black pepper, to taste
For the Salad:
- 200g mixed salad greens
- 1 small red onion, thinly sliced
- 1 small cucumber, diced
- 1 small tomato, diced
- 60g sliced Kalamata olives
- 2 tbsp chopped fresh parsley for garnish

Preparation instructions:
1. Preheat the Air Fryer to 200°C for 5 minutes.
2. In a bowl, combine the olive oil, minced garlic, chopped fresh parsley, dried oregano, salt, and black pepper. This will be the marinade for the octopus.
3. Brush the octopus tentacles with the marinade, ensuring they are evenly coated.
4. Brush the Air Fryer basket with olive oil. Place the marinated octopus tentacles in the Air Fryer basket, ensuring they are not overlapping.
5. Air fry at 200°C for 12-15 minutes or until the octopus is tender and slightly charred, turning once halfway through cooking.
6. While the octopus is cooking, prepare the citrus vinaigrette by whisking together the lemon juice, orange juice, lime juice, extra-virgin olive oil, honey, minced garlic, salt, and black pepper in a small bowl.
7. In a large salad bowl, combine the mixed salad greens, thinly sliced red onion, diced cucumber, diced tomato, and sliced Kalamata olives.
8. Once cooked, remove the grilled octopus from the Air Fryer and let cool for a few minutes. Slice the octopus tentacles into bite-sized pieces.
9. Add the sliced octopus to the salad bowl. Drizzle the citrus vinaigrette over the salad and toss gently to combine.
10. Garnish the grilled octopus salad with chopped fresh parsley.
11. Serve the grilled octopus salad as a refreshing and flavorful appetisers or main course. Enjoy the tender octopus with the bright citrus vinaigrette and crisp salad greens!
12. Note: Adjust the cooking times for the octopus based on its size and tenderness. The given cooking time is an estimate and may vary.

Air Fryer Baja Fish Tacos

Serves: 4
Prep time: 10 minutes / Cook time: 12-15 minutes

Ingredients:
- 4 tilapia fillets, about 140 g each
- 120 g all-purpose flour
- 1 tsp smoked paprika
- 1 tsp garlic powder
- 1 tsp onion powder
- Salt and pepper, to taste
- 1 egg, beaten
- 120ml panko breadcrumbs
- 8 small flour tortillas
- 240ml shredded lettuce
- 1 avocado, diced
- 120ml salsa
- 120 ml sour cream
- 1 lime, cut into wedges

Preparation instructions:
1. Preheat the air fryer to 400°F (200°C).
2. In a large bowl, mix together the flour, paprika, garlic powder, onion powder, salt, and pepper.
3. In another bowl, beat the egg. In a third bowl, add the panko breadcrumbs.
4. Dip each tilapia fillet in the flour mixture, then the egg mixture, and finally the panko breadcrumbs, making sure each side is evenly coated.
5. Place the breaded tilapia fillets in the air fryer basket, making sure they are not touching.
6. Cook for 12-15 minutes, or until the tilapia is golden brown and cooked through.
7. While the tilapia is cooking, warm the tortillas in the microwave for 15-20 seconds or on a dry skillet until they are soft and pliable.
8. To assemble the tacos, place a few pieces of cooked tilapia onto each tortilla.
9. Top with shredded lettuce, diced avocado, salsa, and a dollop of sour cream.
10. Squeeze a wedge of lime over each taco, and serve immediately. Enjoy!

Air Fryer Bang Bang Shrimp with Sweet Chilli Sauce

Serves: 4
Prep time: 10 minutes / Cook time: 8-10 minutes

Ingredients:
- 500 g large shrimp, peeled and deveined
- 100g panko breadcrumbs
- 57 g all-purpose flour
- 2 large eggs, beaten
- Salt and pepper, to taste
- Sweet chilli sauce, to serve

For the sauce:
- 120ml mayonnaise
- 30 ml sweet chilli sauce
- 15 ml rice vinegar
- 1 tsp honey
- 1 clove garlic, minced
- Salt and pepper, to taste

Preparation instructions:
1. In a small bowl, mix together the mayonnaise, sweet chilli sauce, rice vinegar, honey, minced garlic, salt, and pepper. Set aside in the refrigerator.
2. In a shallow dish, mix together the panko breadcrumbs, flour, salt, and pepper.
3. In another shallow dish, beat the eggs.
4. Dip each shrimp into the beaten eggs, then coat with the panko mixture, pressing firmly to adhere.
5. Place the shrimp in a single layer in the basket of your air fryer.
6. Cook at 200°C (400°F) for 8-10 minutes, or until the shrimp are crispy and golden brown.
7. Serve the bang bang shrimp with the sweet chilli sauce for dipping. Enjoy!

Maple Bacon Wrapped Chicken Thighs with Maple Dijon Glaze

Serves: 4
Prep time: 15 minutes / Cook time: 20 minutes

Ingredients:

- 4 chicken thighs, boneless and skinless
- 8 slices of bacon
- 60ml maple syrup
- 2 tbsp Dijon mustard
- 1 tbsp apple cider vinegar
- 1/2 tsp garlic powder
- 1/2 tsp onion powder
- Salt and black pepper, to taste
- Chopped fresh parsley for garnish

Preparation instructions:

1. Preheat the Air Fryer to 200°C for 5 minutes.
2. Season the chicken thighs with salt, black pepper, garlic powder, and onion powder.
3. In a small bowl, whisk together the maple syrup, Dijon mustard, and apple cider vinegar to make the glaze.
4. Wrap each chicken thigh with 2 slices of bacon, securing the bacon with toothpicks if needed.
5. Brush the bacon-wrapped chicken thighs with the maple dijon glaze, reserving some glaze for basting later.
6. Place the chicken thighs in the Air Fryer basket in a single layer, without overcrowding.
7. Air fry at 200°C for 20 minutes, flipping the chicken thighs halfway through cooking.
8. During the last 5 minutes of cooking, brush the chicken thighs with the remaining glaze for a sticky and flavorful finish.
9. Once cooked, remove the chicken thighs from the Air Fryer and let rest for a few minutes.
10. Garnish with chopped fresh parsley before serving. Enjoy the combination of juicy chicken, crispy bacon, and sweet maple dijon glaze!

Jerk Spiced Turkey Burgers with Mango Salsa

Serves: 4
Prep time: 15 minutes / Cook time: 12 minutes

Ingredients:
For the Turkey Burgers:

- 500g ground turkey
- 60g breadcrumbs
- 60g finely chopped red onion
- 60g finely chopped bell pepper
- 2 cloves garlic, minced
- 1 tbsp jerk seasoning
- 1 tsp dried thyme
- 1/2 tsp paprika
- 1/2 tsp salt
- 1/4 tsp black pepper

For the Mango Salsa:

- 1 ripe mango, peeled and diced
- 60g finely chopped red onion
- 60g finely chopped fresh cilantro
- 1 jalapeño pepper, seeded and finely chopped
- Juice of 1 lime
- Salt to taste

For Serving:

- 4 burger buns
- Lettuce leaves
- Sliced tomato
- Sliced red onion

Preparation instructions:

1. Preheat the Air Fryer to 200°C for 5 minutes.
2. In a bowl, combine the ground turkey, breadcrumbs, chopped red onion, chopped bell pepper, minced garlic, jerk seasoning, dried thyme, paprika, salt, and black pepper. Mix well until all the Ingredients are evenly incorporated.
3. Divide the turkey mixture into 4 equal portions and shape each portion into a patty.
4. Place the turkey patties in the Air Fryer basket, without overcrowding.
5. Air fry at 200°C for 12 minutes or until the turkey burgers are cooked through, flipping them halfway through cooking.
6. While the burgers are cooking, prepare the mango salsa by combining the diced mango, chopped red onion, chopped fresh cilantro, jalapeño pepper, lime juice, and salt in a bowl. Mix well and adjust the seasoning to taste.
7. Once cooked, remove the turkey burgers from the

Air Fryer and let rest for a few minutes.

8. Toast the burger buns if desired and assemble the burgers by placing a turkey patty on each bun. Top with lettuce leaves, sliced tomato, sliced red onion, and a generous amount of mango salsa.

9. Serve the jerk spiced turkey burgers with mango salsa for a delicious and tropical twist on a classic burger.

Thai Basil Chicken Lettuce Wraps with Peanut Sauce

Serves: 4
Prep time: 15 minutes / Cook time: 10 minutes

Ingredients:
For the Chicken:
- 500g boneless, skinless chicken breasts, cut into small pieces
- 2 tbsp soy sauce
- 2 tbsp oyster sauce
- 2 tbsp hoisin sauce
- 1 tbsp fish sauce
- 1 tsp brown sugar
- 1/2 tsp cornstarch
- 2 cloves garlic, minced
- 1 red chilli pepper, finely chopped (optional)
- 1 bunch fresh Thai basil leaves, roughly chopped

For the Peanut Sauce:
- 60ml creamy peanut butter
- 2 tbsp soy sauce
- 2 tbsp lime juice
- 1 tbsp honey
- 1 clove garlic, minced
- Water (as needed)

For Serving:
- Lettuce leaves (such as iceberg or butter lettuce)
- Shredded carrots
- Sliced cucumber
- Chopped peanuts
- Lime wedges

Preparation instructions:
1. Preheat the Air Fryer to 200°C for 5 minutes.
2. In a bowl, combine the soy sauce, oyster sauce, hoisin sauce, fish sauce, brown sugar, cornstarch, minced garlic, and chopped red chilli pepper (if using). Mix well to make the marinade.
3. Add the chicken pieces to the marinade and toss to coat evenly. Let the chicken marinate for 10 minutes.

4. While the chicken is marinating, prepare the peanut sauce by combining the creamy peanut butter, soy sauce, lime juice, honey, minced garlic, and water (as needed) in a bowl. Stir well until the sauce reaches a smooth and pourable consistency. Add water gradually to adjust the thickness of the sauce.

5. Place the marinated chicken in the Air Fryer basket, without overcrowding.

6. Air fry at 200°C for 10 minutes or until the chicken is cooked through, stirring or shaking the basket halfway through cooking.

7. Once cooked, remove the chicken from the Air Fryer and stir in the fresh Thai basil leaves while the chicken is still hot.

8. To serve, place a spoonful of the Thai basil chicken mixture onto each lettuce leaf. Top with shredded carrots, sliced cucumber, chopped peanuts, and a drizzle of peanut sauce.

9. Squeeze fresh lime juice over the lettuce wraps before eating. Enjoy the refreshing and flavorful Thai basil chicken lettuce wraps with peanut sauce!

Honey Mustard Glazed Pork Belly Bites with Apple Slaw

Serves: 4
Prep time: 15 minutes / Cook time: 25 minutes

Ingredients:
For the Pork Belly Bites:
- 500g pork belly, cut into bite-sized pieces
- 2 tbsp whole grain mustard
- 2 tbsp honey
- 1 tbsp apple cider vinegar
- 1 tbsp soy sauce
- 1 tsp garlic powder
- 1/2 tsp onion powder
- Salt and black pepper, to taste

For the Apple Slaw:
- 2 apples, julienned
- 60ml mayonnaise
- 1 tbsp apple cider vinegar
- 1 tbsp honey
- 1/2 tsp Dijon mustard
- Salt and black pepper, to taste

Preparation instructions:

1. Preheat the Air Fryer to 200°C for 5 minutes.
2. In a bowl, whisk together the whole grain mustard, honey, apple cider vinegar, soy sauce, garlic powder, onion powder, salt, and black pepper to make the glaze for the pork belly bites.
3. Place the pork belly pieces in a separate bowl and pour the glaze over them. Toss well to coat the pork belly evenly.
4. Arrange the pork belly bites in a single layer in the Air Fryer basket, without overcrowding.
5. Air fry at 200°C for 25 minutes, flipping the pork belly bites halfway through cooking.
6. While the pork belly bites are cooking, prepare the apple slaw by combining the julienned apples, mayonnaise, apple cider vinegar, honey, Dijon mustard, salt, and black pepper in a bowl. Mix well until the apples are coated with the dressing.
7. Once the pork belly bites are cooked and caramelised, remove them from the Air Fryer and let rest for a few minutes.
8. Serve the honey mustard glazed pork belly bites with a side of apple slaw. The combination of sweet and tangy flavours paired with the crispy pork belly bites and refreshing apple slaw is a true delight!

Teriyaki Pineapple Chicken Skewers with Coconut Rice

Serves: 4
Prep time: 20 minutes / Cook time: 15 minutes

Ingredients:
For the Teriyaki Pineapple Chicken Skewers:
- 500g boneless, skinless chicken thighs, cut into bite-sized pieces
- 240g pineapple chunks
- 4 tbsp teriyaki sauce
- 2 tbsp soy sauce
- 2 tbsp honey
- 1 tbsp rice vinegar
- 1/2 tsp garlic powder
- 1/2 tsp onion powder
- Salt and black pepper, to taste
- Wooden skewers, soaked in water for 30 minutes

For the Coconut Rice:
- 240g jasmine rice
- 200ml coconut milk

- 200ml water
- 1/2 tsp salt
- 55g chopped fresh cilantro (optional), for garnish

Preparation instructions:

1. Preheat the Air Fryer to 200°C for 5 minutes.
2. In a bowl, combine the teriyaki sauce, soy sauce, honey, rice vinegar, garlic powder, onion powder, salt, and black pepper to make the marinade for the chicken skewers.
3. Add the chicken thigh pieces to the marinade and toss to coat evenly. Let the chicken marinate for 10 minutes.
4. While the chicken is marinating, prepare the coconut rice. In a saucepan, combine the jasmine rice, coconut milk, water, and salt. Bring to a boil over medium heat, then reduce the heat to low, cover, and simmer for 15 minutes or until the rice is cooked and the liquid is absorbed. Fluff the rice with a fork and garnish with chopped fresh cilantro, if desired.
5. Thread the marinated chicken pieces and pineapple chunks alternately onto the soaked wooden skewers.
6. Place the chicken skewers in the Air Fryer basket, without overcrowding.
7. Air fry at 200°C for 15 minutes or until the chicken is cooked through, flipping the skewers halfway through cooking.
8. Once cooked, remove the chicken skewers from the Air Fryer and let rest for a few minutes.
9. Serve the teriyaki pineapple chicken skewers with a side of coconut rice. The tender and juicy chicken, combined with the sweet and tangy teriyaki glaze and tropical pineapple, pairs perfectly with the fragrant and creamy coconut rice. Enjoy this flavorful and satisfying dish!

Chipotle Lime Grilled Chicken Tacos with Avocado Crema

Serves: 4
Prep time: 20 minutes / Cook time: 12 minutes

Ingredients:
For the Chipotle Lime Grilled Chicken:
- 500g boneless, skinless chicken breasts
- 2 tbsp olive oil
- 2 tbsp lime juice

- 2 cloves garlic, minced
- 1 chipotle pepper in adobo sauce, minced
- 1 tsp ground cumin
- 1/2 tsp chilli powder
- 1/2 tsp smoked paprika
- Salt and black pepper, to taste

For the Avocado Crema:
- 1 ripe avocado
- 60ml sour cream
- 2 tbsp lime juice
- 2 tbsp chopped fresh cilantro
- Salt and black pepper, to taste

For Serving:
- 8 small tortillas
- Sliced red onion
- Chopped fresh cilantro
- Lime wedges

Preparation instructions:

1. In a bowl, whisk together the olive oil, lime juice, minced garlic, minced chipotle pepper, ground cumin, chilli powder, smoked paprika, salt, and black pepper to make the marinade for the chicken.
2. Add the chicken breasts to the marinade and toss to coat evenly. Let the chicken marinate for 10 minutes.
3. Preheat the Air Fryer to 200°C for 5 minutes.
4. Place the marinated chicken breasts in the Air Fryer basket, without overcrowding.
5. Air fry at 200°C for 12 minutes or until the chicken is cooked through, flipping the chicken halfway through cooking.
6. While the chicken is cooking, prepare the avocado crema by combining the ripe avocado, sour cream, lime juice, chopped fresh cilantro, salt, and black pepper in a blender or food processor. Blend until smooth and creamy. Adjust the seasoning to taste.
7. Once cooked, remove the chicken from the Air Fryer and let rest for a few minutes. Then slice the chicken into strips.
8. Warm the tortillas in a dry skillet or microwave.
9. To assemble the tacos, spread a spoonful of avocado crema on each tortilla. Top with sliced chipotle lime grilled chicken, sliced red onion, chopped fresh cilantro, and a squeeze of lime juice.

10. Serve the chipotle lime grilled chicken tacos with avocado crema for a zesty and creamy delight!

Balsamic Fig Glazed Duck Breast with Roasted Root Vegetables

Serves: 4
Prep time: 15 minutes / Cook time: 20 minutes

Ingredients:
For the Balsamic Fig Glazed Duck Breast:
- 4 duck breasts (about 600g)
- 80 ml balsamic vinegar
- 60g fig jam
- 2 tbsp soy sauce
- 2 cloves garlic, minced
- 1 tsp fresh thyme leaves
- Salt and black pepper, to taste

For the Roasted Root Vegetables:
- 500g mixed root vegetables (carrots, parsnips, and potatoes), peeled and cut into chunks
- 2 tbsp olive oil
- 1 tsp dried rosemary
- 1/2 tsp paprika
- Salt and black pepper, to taste

Preparation instructions:

1. Preheat the Air Fryer to 200°C for 5 minutes.
2. In a bowl, whisk together the balsamic vinegar, fig jam, soy sauce, minced garlic, fresh thyme leaves, salt, and black pepper to make the glaze for the duck breasts.
3. Score the skin of the duck breasts in a crisscross pattern. Season both sides of the duck breasts with salt and black pepper.
4. Brush the glaze mixture over the duck breasts, coating them evenly.
5. In a separate bowl, toss the mixed root vegetables with olive oil, dried rosemary, paprika, salt, and black pepper until well coated.
6. Place the duck breasts skin-side down in the Air Fryer basket. Arrange the seasoned root vegetables around the duck breasts.
7. Air fry at 200°C for 10 minutes, then flip the duck breasts and stir the root vegetables.
8. Continue air frying for another 10 minutes or until the duck breasts are cooked to your desired doneness and the vegetables are tender and golden brown.

9. Once cooked, remove the duck breasts and let them rest for a few minutes before slicing.
10. Serve the balsamic fig glazed duck breast slices with the roasted root vegetables for a succulent and flavorful meal.

Cajun Buttermilk Fried Quail with Smoky Remoulade

Serves: 4
Prep time: 20 minutes / Cook time: 15 minutes

Ingredients:
For the Cajun Buttermilk Fried Quail:
- 8 quail, cleaned and halved
- 300ml buttermilk
- 2 tsp Cajun seasoning
- 1 tsp paprika
- 1/2 tsp garlic powder
- 1/2 tsp onion powder
- 1/2 tsp dried thyme
- 1/4 tsp cayenne pepper
- 200g all-purpose flour
- Vegetable oil, for frying
- Salt and black pepper, to taste

For the Smoky Remoulade:
- 120g mayonnaise
- 2 tbsp Dijon mustard
- 1 tbsp smoked paprika
- 1 tbsp chopped fresh parsley
- 1 tbsp chopped fresh chives
- 1 tbsp capers, chopped
- 1 clove garlic, minced
- 1 tsp hot sauce (optional)
- Salt and black pepper, to taste

Preparation instructions:
1. In a bowl, combine the buttermilk, Cajun seasoning, paprika, garlic powder, onion powder, dried thyme, cayenne pepper, salt, and black pepper to make the marinade for the quail.
2. Add the quail halves to the marinade, ensuring they are well coated. Let the quail marinate in the refrigerator for at least 1 hour, or overnight for best results.
3. In a separate bowl, whisk together the all-purpose flour, salt, and black pepper.
4. Preheat the Air Fryer to 200°C for 5 minutes.
5. Remove the quail halves from the marinade,

allowing any excess buttermilk to drip off.
6. Dredge the quail halves in the flour mixture, shaking off any excess.
7. Place the quail halves in the Air Fryer basket in a single layer. Lightly spray or brush the quail with vegetable oil.
8. Air fry at 200°C for 12-15 minutes, turning the quail halfway through cooking, until they are golden brown and cooked through.
9. While the quail is cooking, prepare the smoky remoulade by combining the mayonnaise, Dijon mustard, smoked paprika, chopped fresh parsley, chopped fresh chives, capers, minced garlic, hot sauce (if using), salt, and black pepper in a bowl. Stir until well combined.
10. Once the quail is cooked, serve it hot with the smoky remoulade on the side for dipping. Enjoy the crispy and flavorful Cajun buttermilk fried quail!
11. Note: The cooking time may vary depending on the size of the quail and the air fryer model, so adjust accordingly.

Ginger Soy Glazed Beef Skewers with Sesame Broccoli

Serves: 4
Prep time: 20 minutes / Cook time: 10 minutes

Ingredients:
For the Ginger Soy Glazed Beef Skewers:
- 500g beef sirloin, cut into bite-sized cubes
- 2 tbsp soy sauce
- 2 tbsp hoisin sauce
- 1 tbsp honey
- 1 tbsp grated ginger
- 2 cloves garlic, minced
- 1 tbsp sesame oil
- 1 tbsp vegetable oil
- Salt and black pepper, to taste
- 4-5 skewers, soaked in water if using wooden skewers

For the Sesame Broccoli:
- 400g broccoli florets
- 1 tbsp sesame oil
- 1 tbsp soy sauce
- 1 tbsp toasted sesame seeds

Preparation instructions:

1. In a bowl, combine the soy sauce, hoisin sauce, honey, grated ginger, minced garlic, sesame oil, vegetable oil, salt, and black pepper to make the marinade for the beef skewers.
2. Add the beef cubes to the marinade, ensuring they are well coated. Let the beef marinate for at least 15 minutes.
3. Preheat the Air Fryer to 200°C for 5 minutes.
4. Thread the marinated beef cubes onto the skewers, leaving a small gap between each piece.
5. Place the beef skewers in the Air Fryer basket and air fry at 200°C for 8-10 minutes, turning them halfway through cooking, until the beef is cooked to your desired doneness.
6. While the beef skewers are cooking, steam the broccoli florets until they are tender but still crisp.
7. In a separate bowl, whisk together the sesame oil and soy sauce for the sesame broccoli.
8. Toss the steamed broccoli in the sesame oil and soy sauce mixture until well coated. Sprinkle it with toasted sesame seeds.
9. Once the beef skewers are cooked, serve them with the sesame broccoli on the side. Enjoy the succulent ginger soy glazed beef with the flavorful sesame broccoli.

Vietnamese Lemongrass Grilled Pork with Rice Vermicelli Salad

Serves: 4
Prep time: 30 minutes / Cook time: 10 minutes

Ingredients:
For the Lemongrass Grilled Pork:
- 500g pork tenderloin, thinly sliced
- 3 tbsp lemongrass, finely chopped
- 3 cloves garlic, minced
- 2 tbsp fish sauce
- 2 tbsp soy sauce
- 1 tbsp honey
- 1 tbsp vegetable oil
- 1 tsp five-spice powder (optional)
- Salt and black pepper, to taste

For the Rice Vermicelli Salad:
- 200g rice vermicelli noodles
- 240g mixed salad greens
- 1 carrot, julienned

- 1 cucumber, thinly sliced
- 60g fresh mint leaves
- 60g fresh cilantro leaves
- 60g chopped roasted peanuts
- Lime wedges, for serving

Preparation instructions:

1. In a bowl, combine the lemongrass, minced garlic, fish sauce, soy sauce, honey, vegetable oil, five-spice powder (if using), salt, and black pepper to make the marinade for the grilled pork.
2. Add the sliced pork tenderloin to the marinade, ensuring it is well coated. Let the pork marinate for at least 20 minutes.
3. Cook the rice vermicelli noodles according to the package instructions. Drain and rinse with cold water to stop the cooking process. Set aside.
4. Preheat the Air Fryer to 200°C for 5 minutes.
5. Thread the marinated pork slices onto skewers, leaving a small gap between each piece.
6. Place the pork skewers in the Air Fryer basket and air fry at 200°C for 8-10 minutes, turning them halfway through cooking, until the pork is cooked through and slightly charred.
7. In a large bowl, combine the cooked rice vermicelli noodles, mixed salad greens, julienned carrot, thinly sliced cucumber, fresh mint leaves, and fresh cilantro leaves. Toss to mix well.
8. To serve, divide the rice vermicelli salad among plates. Top with the grilled pork skewers. Sprinkle with chopped roasted peanuts and serve with lime wedges on the side. Enjoy the vibrant flavours of the Vietnamese lemongrass grilled pork with the refreshing rice vermicelli salad.

Garlic Parmesan Turkey Meatballs with Marinara Sauce

Serves: 4
Prep time: 20 minutes / Cook time: 15 minutes

Ingredients:
For the Garlic Parmesan Turkey Meatballs:
- 500g ground turkey
- 120g breadcrumbs
- 60g grated Parmesan cheese
- 2 cloves garlic, minced
- 2 tbsp chopped fresh parsley
- 1 large egg

- 1/4 tsp dried oregano
- 1/4 tsp dried basil
- Salt and black pepper, to taste
- 1 tbsp olive oil

For the Marinara Sauce:
- 400g canned crushed tomatoes
- 2 cloves garlic, minced
- 1 tbsp tomato paste
- 1 tbsp olive oil
- 1 tsp dried basil
- 1 tsp dried oregano
- 1/2 tsp sugar
- Salt and black pepper, to taste

Preparation instructions:
1. In a bowl, combine the ground turkey, breadcrumbs, grated Parmesan cheese, minced garlic, chopped fresh parsley, egg, dried oregano, dried basil, salt, and black pepper to make the turkey meatball mixture.
2. Mix the Ingredients together until well combined. Shape the mixture into meatballs of desired size.
3. Preheat the Air Fryer to 200°C for 5 minutes.
4. Place the meatballs in the Air Fryer basket, ensuring they are not touching each other. Drizzle the meatballs with olive oil.
5. Air fry at 200°C for 12-15 minutes, shaking the basket or turning the meatballs halfway through cooking, until they are browned and cooked through.
6. While the meatballs are cooking, prepare the marinara sauce. In a saucepan, heat the olive oil over medium heat. Add the minced garlic and sauté until fragrant.
7. Add the canned crushed tomatoes, tomato paste, dried basil, dried oregano, sugar, salt, and black pepper to the saucepan. Stir to combine.
8. Simmer the marinara sauce over low heat for 10 minutes, allowing the flavours to meld together.
9. Once the meatballs are cooked, transfer them to a serving dish and pour the marinara sauce over them. Serve the garlic Parmesan turkey meatballs with the marinara sauce. They are delicious on their own or served with pasta or crusty bread.
10. Note: The cooking time may vary depending on the size of the meatballs and the air fryer model, so adjust accordingly.

Sriracha Honey Glazed Duck Wings with Pickled Vegetables

Serves: 4
Prep time: 20 minutes / Cook time: 25 minutes

Ingredients:
For the Sriracha Honey Glazed Duck Wings:
- 800g duck wings
- 2 tbsp sriracha sauce
- 2 tbsp honey
- 2 tbsp soy sauce
- 2 cloves garlic, minced
- 1 tbsp vegetable oil
- Salt and black pepper, to taste
- 2 green onions, thinly sliced (for garnish)

For the Pickled Vegetables:
- 1 carrot, julienned
- 1 daikon radish, julienned
- 60ml rice vinegar
- 1 tbsp sugar
- 1/2 tsp salt

Preparation instructions:
1. In a bowl, combine the sriracha sauce, honey, soy sauce, minced garlic, vegetable oil, salt, and black pepper to make the glaze for the duck wings.
2. Add the duck wings to the glaze, ensuring they are well coated. Let the wings marinate for at least 15 minutes.
3. Preheat the Air Fryer to 200°C for 5 minutes.
4. Place the marinated duck wings in the Air Fryer basket, leaving a small gap between each wing.
5. Air fry at 200°C for 20-25 minutes, turning the wings halfway through cooking, until they are crispy and cooked through.
6. While the duck wings are cooking, prepare the pickled vegetables. In a bowl, combine the julienned carrot, julienned daikon radish, rice vinegar, sugar, and salt. Mix well and let the vegetables pickle for at least 10 minutes.
7. Once the duck wings are cooked, transfer them to a serving dish. Sprinkle with thinly sliced green onions for garnish.
8. Serve the sriracha honey glazed duck wings with the pickled vegetables on the side. The combination of sweet, spicy, and tangy flavours will tantalise your taste buds.
9. Enjoy!

Panko Crusted Pork Schnitzel with Lemon-Caper Butter Sauce

Serves: 4
Prep time: 15 minutes / Cook time: 12 minutes

Ingredients:

For the Pork Schnitzel:
- 4 pork loin steaks (about 150g each)
- 80g all-purpose flour
- 2 large eggs
- 120g panko breadcrumbs
- 1/2 tsp paprika
- Salt and black pepper, to taste
- Vegetable oil, for frying

For the Lemon-Caper Butter Sauce:
- 60g unsalted butter
- 1 tbsp lemon juice
- 2 tbsp capers, drained
- 2 tbsp chopped fresh parsley

Preparation instructions:

1. Place the pork loin steaks between two sheets of plastic wrap and pound them with a meat mallet until they are about 1/4 inch thick.
2. Set up a breading station with three shallow bowls. In the first bowl, place the flour. In the second bowl, beat the eggs. In the third bowl, combine the panko breadcrumbs, paprika, salt, and black pepper.
3. Dip each pork loin steak into the flour, shaking off any excess. Then dip it into the beaten eggs, allowing any excess to drip off. Finally, coat the steak with the panko breadcrumb mixture, pressing gently to adhere.
4. Preheat the Air Fryer to 200°C for 5 minutes.
5. Place the breaded pork schnitzel in the Air Fryer basket in a single layer, without overcrowding.
6. Air fry at 200°C for 10-12 minutes, flipping the schnitzel halfway through cooking, until they are golden brown and crispy.
7. While the schnitzel is cooking, prepare the lemon-caper butter sauce. In a small saucepan, melt the butter over low heat. Stir in the lemon juice, capers, and chopped fresh parsley. Keep warm until ready to serve.
8. Once the pork schnitzel is cooked, remove them from the Air Fryer and let them rest for a few minutes.
9. Serve the panko crusted pork schnitzel with a drizzle of the lemon-caper butter sauce. It pairs well with a side of mashed potatoes or a fresh salad.

Spicy Jamaican Jerk Chicken Sliders with Pineapple Slaw

Serves: 4
Prep time: 20 minutes + marinating time / Cook time: 12 minutes

Ingredients:

For the Jerk Chicken:
- 500g boneless, skinless chicken breasts
- 2 tbsp Jamaican jerk seasoning
- 2 tbsp olive oil

For the Pineapple Slaw:
- 200g shredded cabbage
- 100g diced pineapple
- 2 green onions, thinly sliced
- 2 tbsp mayonnaise
- 1 tbsp apple cider vinegar
- 1 tsp honey
- Salt and black pepper, to taste

For the Sliders:
- 8 small slider buns
- Sliced tomatoes and lettuce, for serving

Preparation instructions:

1. Slice the chicken breasts into thin cutlets to ensure quick and even cooking.
2. In a bowl, combine the Jamaican jerk seasoning and olive oil. Add the chicken cutlets to the bowl and toss to coat them evenly in the seasoning. Let the chicken marinate for at least 1 hour or overnight in the refrigerator.
3. Preheat the Air Fryer to 200°C for 5 minutes.
4. Place the marinated chicken cutlets in the Air Fryer basket, ensuring they are not touching each other.
5. Air fry at 200°C for 10-12 minutes, flipping the chicken halfway through cooking, until it is cooked through and slightly charred.
6. While the chicken is cooking, prepare the pineapple slaw. In a bowl, combine the shredded cabbage, diced pineapple, thinly sliced green

onions, mayonnaise, apple cider vinegar, honey, salt, and black pepper. Toss well to combine.

7. Once the chicken is cooked, remove it from the Air Fryer and let it rest for a few minutes.

8. To assemble the sliders, slice the slider buns in half. Place a chicken cutlet on the bottom half of each bun. Top with a spoonful of pineapple slaw, sliced tomatoes, and lettuce. Place the top half of the bun on top.

9. Serve the spicy Jamaican jerk chicken sliders with pineapple slaw as a delicious and flavorful meal.

Moroccan Spiced Grilled Lamb Kebabs with Mint Yoghurt Sauce

Serves: 4

Prep time: 20 minutes + marinating time / Cook time: 10 minutes

Ingredients:
For the Lamb Kebabs:
- 500g lamb leg or shoulder, cut into 1-inch cubes
- 2 tbsp olive oil
- 2 cloves garlic, minced
- 1 tsp ground cumin
- 1 tsp ground coriander
- 1/2 tsp ground paprika
- 1/2 tsp ground cinnamon
- 1/2 tsp ground ginger
- Salt and black pepper, to taste

For the Mint Yoghurt Sauce:
- 200g plain Greek yoghurt
- 2 tbsp chopped fresh mint leaves
- 1 tbsp lemon juice
- 1 clove garlic, minced
- Salt, to taste

Preparation instructions:
1. In a bowl, combine the olive oil, minced garlic, ground cumin, ground coriander, ground paprika, ground cinnamon, ground ginger, salt, and black pepper to make the marinade for the lamb kebabs.

2. Add the lamb cubes to the bowl and toss to coat them evenly in the marinade. Let the lamb marinate for at least 1 hour or overnight in the refrigerator.

3. Preheat the Air Fryer to 200°C for 5 minutes.

4. Thread the marinated lamb cubes onto skewers, leaving a small gap between each piece.

5. Place the lamb kebabs in the Air Fryer basket, ensuring they are not touching each other.

6. Air fry at 200°C for 8-10 minutes, turning the kebabs halfway through cooking, until they are cooked to your desired level of doneness.

7. While the lamb kebabs are cooking, prepare the mint yoghurt sauce. In a bowl, combine the plain Greek yoghurt, chopped fresh mint leaves, lemon juice, minced garlic, and salt. Mix well.

8. Once the lamb kebabs are cooked, remove them from the Air Fryer and let them rest for a few minutes.

9. Serve the Moroccan spiced grilled lamb kebabs with the mint yoghurt sauce on the side. They are best enjoyed with warm flatbread and a fresh salad.

Szechuan Peppercorn Crusted Beef Stir-Fry with Vegetables

Serves: 4

Prep time: 15 minutes / Cook time: 10 minutes

Ingredients:
For the Beef Stir-Fry:
- 500g beef sirloin, thinly sliced
- 2 tbsp soy sauce
- 2 tbsp cornstarch
- 2 tsp Szechuan peppercorns, crushed
- 1 tsp Chinese five-spice powder
- 2 tbsp vegetable oil
- 2 cloves garlic, minced
- 1 red bell pepper, thinly sliced
- 1 yellow bell pepper, thinly sliced
- 1 carrot, julienned
- 150g sugar snap peas
- 4 spring onions, sliced
- Salt and black pepper, to taste

For the Stir-Fry Sauce:
- 60ml soy sauce
- 60ml water
- 2 tbsp oyster sauce
- 2 tbsp rice vinegar
- 1 tbsp honey
- 1 tsp sesame oil

Preparation instructions:

1. In a bowl, combine the soy sauce, cornstarch, crushed Szechuan peppercorns, and Chinese five-spice powder to make a marinade for the beef.
2. Add the sliced beef to the bowl and toss to coat it evenly in the marinade. Let the beef marinate for 10-15 minutes.
3. In a separate bowl, whisk together the soy sauce, water, oyster sauce, rice vinegar, honey, and sesame oil to make the stir-fry sauce. Set aside.
4. Preheat the Air Fryer to 200°C for 5 minutes.
5. Heat the vegetable oil in a wok or large frying pan over high heat. Add the minced garlic and stir-fry for a few seconds until fragrant.
6. Add the marinated beef to the wok and stir-fry for 3-4 minutes until it is browned and cooked to your desired level of doneness. Remove the beef from the wok and set it aside.
7. In the same wok, add the sliced red and yellow bell peppers, julienned carrot, sugar snap peas, and sliced spring onions. Stir-fry for 3-4 minutes until the vegetables are crisp-tender.
8. Return the cooked beef to the wok and pour in the stir-fry sauce. Stir-fry for another 1-2 minutes until the sauce coats the beef and vegetables.
9. Season with salt and black pepper to taste.
10. Once the stir-fry is ready, remove it from the heat and serve immediately.
11. Enjoy the Szechuan peppercorn crusted beef stir-fry with vegetables with steamed rice or noodles.

Honey Sriracha Glazed Bacon Wrapped Turkey Breast with Roasted Vegetables

Serves: 4
Prep time: 20 minutes / Cook time: 35 minutes

Ingredients:
For the Turkey Breast:
- 500g boneless, skinless turkey breast
- 8 slices bacon
- 2 tbsp honey
- 1 tbsp sriracha sauce
- 1 tbsp olive oil
- 1 clove garlic, minced
- 1 tsp smoked paprika
- Salt and black pepper, to taste

For the Roasted Vegetables:
- 400g baby potatoes, halved
- 200g carrots, cut into sticks
- 200g parsnips, cut into sticks
- 2 tbsp olive oil
- 1 tsp dried thyme
- Salt and black pepper, to taste

Preparation instructions:

1. Preheat the Air Fryer to 190°C for 5 minutes.
2. Place the boneless, skinless turkey breast on a cutting board. Season it with salt and black pepper.
3. In a small bowl, combine the honey, sriracha sauce, olive oil, minced garlic, smoked paprika, salt, and black pepper to make the glaze for the turkey.
4. Brush the glaze all over the turkey breast, ensuring it is well coated.
5. Wrap the turkey breast with the bacon slices, tucking the ends underneath.
6. In a separate bowl, toss the halved baby potatoes, carrot sticks, and parsnip sticks with olive oil, dried thyme, salt, and black pepper to coat them evenly.
7. Place the bacon-wrapped turkey breast and the seasoned vegetables in the Air Fryer basket, ensuring they are in a single layer without overcrowding.
8. Air fry at 190°C for 30-35 minutes, turning the turkey breast and stirring the vegetables halfway through cooking, until the turkey is cooked through and the vegetables are tender and golden brown.
9. Once cooked, remove the turkey breast and vegetables from the Air Fryer and let them rest for a few minutes.
10. Slice the turkey breast and serve it with the roasted vegetables.
11. Enjoy the honey sriracha glazed bacon wrapped turkey breast with roasted vegetables as a delicious and flavorful meal.

18 Mango Habanero Glazed Pork Tenderloin with Grilled Pineapple Salsa

Serves: 4
Prep time: 20 minutes + marinating time / Cook time: 15 minutes

Ingredients:
For the Pork Tenderloin:
* 500g pork tenderloin
* 4 tbsp mango habanero sauce
* 2 tbsp soy sauce
* 2 tbsp lime juice
* 2 cloves garlic, minced
* 1 tbsp olive oil
* Salt and black pepper, to taste

For the Grilled Pineapple Salsa:
* 1 ripe pineapple, peeled, cored, and sliced
* 1 red bell pepper, diced
* 1 small red onion, diced
* 1 jalapeno pepper, seeded and minced
* 2 tbsp chopped fresh cilantro
* 2 tbsp lime juice
* Salt, to taste

Preparation instructions:
1. In a bowl, combine the mango habanero sauce, soy sauce, lime juice, minced garlic, olive oil, salt, and black pepper to make the marinade for the pork tenderloin.
2. Place the pork tenderloin in a resealable plastic bag or shallow dish. Pour the marinade over the pork, ensuring it is well coated. Let the pork marinate for at least 1 hour or overnight in the refrigerator.
3. Preheat the Air Fryer to 200°C for 5 minutes.
4. Remove the pork tenderloin from the marinade and discard the excess marinade.
5. Place the pork tenderloin in the Air Fryer basket.
6. Air fry at 200°C for 12-15 minutes, turning the pork halfway through cooking, until it reaches an internal temperature of 63°C.
7. While the pork tenderloin is cooking, prepare the grilled pineapple salsa. Preheat a grill or grill pan over high heat. Grill the pineapple slices for 2-3 minutes per side until they are slightly charred. Remove from the grill and let them cool. Dice the grilled pineapple and combine it with the diced red bell pepper, diced red onion, minced jalapeno pepper, chopped fresh cilantro, lime juice, and salt in a bowl. Mix well.
8. Once the pork tenderloin is cooked, remove it from the Air Fryer and let it rest for a few minutes.
9. Slice the pork tenderloin and serve it with the grilled pineapple salsa.
10. Enjoy the mango habanero glazed pork tenderloin with grilled pineapple salsa as a delightful and tangy dish.

Pineapple Chicken Skewers

Serves: 2 people
Prep time: 15-20 minutes | Cook time: 10-12 minutes

Ingredients:
* 400g boneless, skinless chicken breast, cut into chunks
* 200g fresh pineapple, cut into chunks
* 30 ml soy sauce
* 15 ml honey
* 15 ml olive oil
* 5g garlic powder
* Salt and pepper to taste
* Wooden skewers, soaked in water for 30 minutes

Preparation instructions:
1. Preheat the air fryer to 200°C (400°F).
2. In a bowl, whisk together the soy sauce, honey, olive oil, garlic powder, salt, and pepper.
3. Add the chicken breast chunks to the bowl and toss until well-coated with the marinade. Let it marinate for at least 15 minutes.
4. Thread the marinated chicken and pineapple chunks onto the soaked wooden skewers, alternating between chicken and pineapple.
5. Place the skewers in a single layer in the air fryer basket.
6. Air fry for 10-12 minutes, flipping the skewers halfway through, until the chicken is cooked through and the pineapple is caramelised.
7. Remove from the air fryer and serve hot as a delightful appetiser or main dish.

Chapter 5: Healthy Vegetables & Fruit

Cinnamon Roasted Butternut Squash Wedges with Greek Yoghurt Dip

Serves: 4
Prep time: 10 minutes / Cook time: 20 minutes

Ingredients:
- 500g butternut squash, peeled, seeded, and cut into wedges
- 2 tbsp olive oil
- 1 tbsp maple syrup
- 1 tsp ground cinnamon
- 1/2 tsp ground nutmeg
- Salt, to taste

For the Greek Yoghurt Dip:
- 200g Greek yoghurt
- 1 tbsp lemon juice
- 1 tbsp chopped fresh dill
- 1 clove garlic, minced
- Salt and black pepper, to taste

Preparation instructions:
1. Preheat the Air Fryer to 200°C for 5 minutes.
2. In a bowl, combine the olive oil, maple syrup, ground cinnamon, ground nutmeg, and salt. Whisk together to make a marinade.
3. Add the butternut squash wedges to the bowl and toss to coat them evenly in the marinade.
4. Place the butternut squash wedges in the Air Fryer basket, ensuring they are in a single layer without overcrowding.
5. Air fry at 200°C for 18-20 minutes, flipping the wedges halfway through cooking, until they are tender and caramelised.
6. While the butternut squash is cooking, prepare the Greek yoghurt dip. In a separate bowl, combine the Greek yoghurt, lemon juice, chopped fresh dill, minced garlic, salt, and black pepper. Mix well.
7. Once the butternut squash wedges are cooked, remove them from the Air Fryer and let them cool for a few minutes.
8. Serve the cinnamon roasted butternut squash wedges with the Greek yoghurt dip on the side.
9. Enjoy the sweet and aromatic flavours of the butternut squash with the cool and tangy Greek yoghurt dip.

Coconut Lime Brussels Sprouts with Toasted Coconut Flakes

Serves: 4
Prep time: 10 minutes / Cook time: 15 minutes

Ingredients:
- 500g Brussels sprouts, trimmed and halved
- 2 tbsp coconut oil, melted
- 1 tbsp lime juice
- 1 tsp lime zest
- 2 tbsp desiccated coconut
- Salt and black pepper, to taste

Preparation instructions:
1. Preheat the Air Fryer to 180°C for 5 minutes.
2. In a bowl, combine the melted coconut oil, lime juice, lime zest, salt, and black pepper. Whisk together to make a dressing.
3. Add the Brussels sprouts to the bowl and toss to coat them evenly in the dressing.
4. Place the Brussels sprouts in the Air Fryer basket, ensuring they are in a single layer without overcrowding.
5. Air fry at 180°C for 12-15 minutes, shaking the basket halfway through cooking, until the Brussels sprouts are crispy and golden brown.
6. While the Brussels sprouts are cooking, heat a dry skillet over medium heat. Add the desiccated coconut and toast it for 2-3 minutes until it turns golden brown. Stir frequently to prevent burning.
7. Once the Brussels sprouts are cooked, remove them from the Air Fryer and sprinkle the toasted coconut flakes over them.
8. Serve the coconut lime Brussels sprouts as a flavorful and tropical side dish.
9. Enjoy the combination of crispy Brussels sprouts with the refreshing flavours of coconut and lime.

Balsamic Glazed Portobello Mushroom Caps with Goat Cheese

Serves: 4
Prep time: 10 minutes / Cook time: 12 minutes

Ingredients:

- 4 large Portobello mushroom caps
- 2 tbsp balsamic vinegar
- 2 tbsp olive oil
- 2 cloves garlic, minced
- 1 tsp dried thyme
- Salt and black pepper, to taste
- 100g goat cheese, crumbled
- 2 tbsp chopped fresh parsley

Preparation instructions:

1. Preheat the Air Fryer to 180°C for 5 minutes.
2. In a small bowl, whisk together the balsamic vinegar, olive oil, minced garlic, dried thyme, salt, and black pepper to make the glaze.
3. Brush both sides of the Portobello mushroom caps with the glaze, ensuring they are well coated.
4. Place the mushroom caps in the Air Fryer basket, gill-side up.
5. Air fry at 180°C for 10-12 minutes until the mushrooms are tender and the glaze has thickened.
6. Remove the mushroom caps from the Air Fryer and crumble goat cheese over each cap.
7. Return the mushroom caps to the Air Fryer and air fry for an additional 2 minutes until the cheese has softened.
8. Sprinkle the chopped fresh parsley over the mushroom caps.
9. Serve the balsamic glazed Portobello mushroom caps with goat cheese as a delightful appetiser or main dish.
10. Enjoy the savoury and tangy flavours of the glazed mushrooms with the creamy goat cheese.

Maple Sriracha Roasted Carrot Fries with Greek Yogurt Ranch

Serves: 4
Prep time: 10 minutes / Cook time: 15 minutes

Ingredients:

- 500g carrots, peeled and cut into fries
- 2 tbsp olive oil
- 2 tbsp maple syrup
- 1 tbsp sriracha sauce
- 1/2 tsp smoked paprika
- Salt and black pepper, to taste

For the Greek Yoghurt Ranch:

- 200g Greek yoghurt
- 1 tbsp chopped fresh dill
- 1 tbsp chopped fresh chives
- 1 clove garlic, minced
- 1 tbsp lemon juice
- Salt and black pepper, to taste

Preparation instructions:

1. Preheat the Air Fryer to 200°C for 5 minutes.
2. In a bowl, whisk together the olive oil, maple syrup, sriracha sauce, smoked paprika, salt, and black pepper to make the marinade.
3. Add the carrot fries to the bowl and toss to coat them evenly in the marinade.
4. Place the carrot fries in the Air Fryer basket, ensuring they are in a single layer without overcrowding.
5. Air fry at 200°C for 12-15 minutes, shaking the basket halfway through cooking, until the carrot fries are crispy and caramelised.
6. While the carrot fries are cooking, prepare the Greek yoghurt ranch. In a separate bowl, combine the Greek yoghurt, chopped fresh dill, chopped fresh chives, minced garlic, lemon juice, salt, and black pepper. Mix well.
7. Once the carrot fries are cooked, remove them from the Air Fryer and let them cool for a few minutes.
8. Serve the maple sriracha roasted carrot fries with the Greek yoghurt ranch on the side.
9. Enjoy the sweet and spicy flavours of the carrot fries with the cool and creamy Greek yoghurt ranch.

Spiralized Sweet Potato Noodles with Garlic Parmesan Sauce

Serves: 4
Prep time: 10 minutes / Cook time: 15 minutes

Ingredients:

- 2 large sweet potatoes
- 2 tbsp olive oil
- 2 cloves garlic, minced
- 120g grated Parmesan cheese
- 60g chopped fresh parsley
- Salt and black pepper, to taste

Preparation instructions:

1. Preheat the Air Fryer to 200°C for 5 minutes.
2. Peel the sweet potatoes and spiralize them using a spiralizer to create noodles.
3. In a bowl, toss the sweet potato noodles with olive

oil, minced garlic, salt, and black pepper.

4. Place the sweet potato noodles in the Air Fryer basket, ensuring they are in a single layer without overcrowding.

5. Air fry at 200°C for 12-15 minutes, shaking the basket halfway through cooking, until the sweet potato noodles are tender and slightly crispy.

6. Once the sweet potato noodles are cooked, remove them from the Air Fryer and transfer them to a serving dish.

7. In a small saucepan, melt the grated Parmesan cheese over low heat until it becomes a smooth sauce.

8. Pour the garlic Parmesan sauce over the sweet potato noodles and toss to coat them evenly.

9. Sprinkle the chopped fresh parsley over the noodles for added freshness and flavour.

10. Serve the spiralized sweet potato noodles with garlic Parmesan sauce as a delicious and healthy side dish or light main course.

11. Enjoy the satisfying and cheesy taste of the sweet potato noodles with the aromatic garlic Parmesan sauce.

Sesame Ginger Green Beans with Toasted Almonds

Serves: 4
Prep time: 10 minutes / Cook time: 10 minutes

Ingredients:

- 400g green beans, trimmed
- 2 tbsp sesame oil
- 2 tbsp soy sauce
- 1 tbsp rice vinegar
- 1 tbsp honey
- 1 tbsp grated fresh ginger
- 2 cloves garlic, minced
- 2 tbsp toasted sesame seeds
- 50g toasted almonds, chopped
- Salt and black pepper, to taste

Preparation instructions:

1. Preheat the Air Fryer to 180°C for 5 minutes.

2. In a small bowl, whisk together the sesame oil, soy sauce, rice vinegar, honey, grated fresh ginger, minced garlic, salt, and black pepper to make the sauce.

3. Place the green beans in the Air Fryer basket, ensuring they are in a single layer without

overcrowding.

4. Air fry at 180°C for 8-10 minutes until the green beans are tender-crisp and slightly charred.

5. Once the green beans are cooked, transfer them to a serving dish.

6. Pour the sauce over the green beans and toss to coat them evenly.

7. Sprinkle the toasted sesame seeds and chopped toasted almonds over the green beans for added crunch and nuttiness.

8. Serve the sesame ginger green beans with toasted almonds as a flavorful and nutritious side dish.

9. Enjoy the vibrant flavours of the green beans combined with the aromatic sesame ginger sauce and crunchy almonds.

Crispy Parmesan Roasted Broccoli Bites

Serves: 4
Prep time: 10 minutes / Cook time: 15 minutes

Ingredients:

- 500g broccoli florets
- 2 tbsp olive oil
- 120g grated Parmesan cheese
- 1/2 tsp garlic powder
- 1/2 tsp onion powder
- Salt and black pepper, to taste

Preparation instructions:

1. Preheat the Air Fryer to 200°C for 5 minutes.

2. In a bowl, toss the broccoli florets with olive oil, grated Parmesan cheese, garlic powder, onion powder, salt, and black pepper.

3. Place the broccoli florets in the Air Fryer basket, ensuring they are in a single layer without overcrowding.

4. Air fry at 200°C for 12-15 minutes until the broccoli is crispy and the Parmesan cheese is golden brown.

5. Once the broccoli bites are cooked, remove them from the Air Fryer and let them cool for a few minutes.

6. Serve the crispy Parmesan roasted broccoli bites as a tasty and healthy appetiser or side dish.

7. Enjoy the delightful combination of crispy broccoli with the savoury flavours of Parmesan cheese and aromatic spices.

Mango Habanero Glazed Pineapple Skewers

Serves: 4
Prep time: 15 minutes / Cook time: 10 minutes

Ingredients:
- 1 medium pineapple, peeled, cored, and cut into chunks
- For the Mango Habanero Glaze:
- 200g mango, peeled and diced
- 1 habanero pepper, seeded and minced
- 2 tbsp lime juice
- 2 tbsp honey
- 1/4 tsp salt

Preparation instructions:
1. Preheat the Air Fryer to 200°C for 5 minutes.
2. Thread the pineapple chunks onto skewers.
3. In a blender or food processor, combine the diced mango, minced habanero pepper, lime juice, honey, and salt. Blend until smooth to make the glaze.
4. Brush the mango habanero glaze over the pineapple skewers, coating them evenly.
5. Place the pineapple skewers in the Air Fryer basket, ensuring they are in a single layer without overcrowding.
6. Air fry at 200°C for 8-10 minutes until the pineapple is caramelised and slightly charred.
7. Once the pineapple skewers are cooked, remove them from the Air Fryer and let them cool for a few minutes.
8. Serve the mango habanero glazed pineapple skewers as a spicy and tropical dessert or appetiser.
9. Enjoy the combination of sweet and tangy mango glaze with the natural sweetness of the caramelised pineapple.

Garlic Rosemary Roasted Root Vegetable Medley

Serves: 4
Prep time: 10 minutes / Cook time: 25 minutes

Ingredients:
- 400g mixed root vegetables (such as carrots, parsnips, and turnips), peeled and cut into chunks
- 2 tbsp olive oil
- 3 cloves garlic, minced
- 1 tbsp chopped fresh rosemary
- Salt and black pepper, to taste

Preparation instructions:
1. Preheat the Air Fryer to 200°C for 5 minutes.
2. In a bowl, toss the mixed root vegetables with olive oil, minced garlic, chopped fresh rosemary, salt, and black pepper.
3. Place the root vegetable chunks in the Air Fryer basket, ensuring they are in a single layer without overcrowding.
4. Air fry at 200°C for 20-25 minutes until the vegetables are tender and caramelised, stirring them halfway through cooking.
5. Once the root vegetable medley is cooked, remove it from the Air Fryer and let it cool for a few minutes.
6. Serve the garlic rosemary roasted root vegetable medley as a hearty and flavorful side dish.
7. Enjoy the earthy and aromatic flavours of the roasted root vegetables with hints of garlic and rosemary.

Turmeric Infused Roasted Eggplant Rounds with Mint Yogurt Sauce

Serves: 4
Prep time: 15 minutes / Cook time: 20 minutes

Ingredients:
- 2 large eggplants, sliced into rounds
- 2 tbsp olive oil
- 1 tsp ground turmeric
- 1/2 tsp ground cumin
- 1/2 tsp ground coriander
- Salt and black pepper, to taste

For the Mint Yoghurt Sauce:
- 200g Greek yoghurt
- 2 tbsp chopped fresh mint
- 1 tbsp lemon juice
- 1 clove garlic, minced
- Salt and black pepper, to taste

Preparation instructions:
1. Preheat the Air Fryer to 200°C for 5 minutes.
2. In a small bowl, combine the olive oil, ground turmeric, ground cumin, ground coriander, salt, and black pepper to make a marinade.
3. Brush both sides of the eggplant rounds with the marinade, ensuring they are well coated.
4. Place the eggplant rounds in the Air Fryer basket,

ensuring they are in a single layer without overlapping.

5. Air fry at 200°C for 18-20 minutes until the eggplant is tender and golden brown, flipping the rounds halfway through cooking.

6. While the eggplant is cooking, prepare the mint yoghurt sauce. In a separate bowl, combine the Greek yoghurt, chopped fresh mint, lemon juice, minced garlic, salt, and black pepper. Mix well.

7. Once the eggplant rounds are cooked, remove them from the Air Fryer and let them cool for a few minutes.

8. Serve the turmeric-infused roasted eggplant rounds with the mint yoghurt sauce on the side.

9. Enjoy the fragrant and spiced flavours of the roasted eggplant paired with the refreshing mint yoghurt sauce.

Strawberry Balsamic Bruschetta with Basil and Toasted Baguette Slices

Serves: 4
Prep time: 10 minutes / Cook time: 5 minutes

Ingredients:

- 200g strawberries, diced
- 2 tbsp balsamic vinegar
- 1 tbsp honey
- 1 tbsp fresh basil, finely chopped
- 4 slices of baguette
- 1 tbsp olive oil

Preparation instructions:

1. Preheat the Air Fryer to 180°C for 5 minutes.

2. In a bowl, combine the diced strawberries, balsamic vinegar, honey, and fresh basil. Mix well and set aside to marinate.

3. Brush the baguette slices with olive oil on both sides.

4. Place the baguette slices in the Air Fryer basket, ensuring they are in a single layer without overcrowding.

5. Air fry at 180°C for 3-5 minutes until the baguette slices are crispy and golden brown.

6. Once the baguette slices are cooked, remove them from the Air Fryer and let them cool for a few minutes.

7. Top each baguette slice with a spoonful of the strawberry balsamic mixture.

8. Serve the strawberry balsamic bruschetta as a delightful appetiser or snack.

9. Enjoy the sweet and tangy flavours of the marinated strawberries paired with the fresh basil on crispy toasted baguette slices.

Smoky Paprika Roasted Bell Pepper Strips with Cilantro Lime Sauce

Serves: 4
Prep time: 10 minutes / Cook time: 15 minutes

Ingredients:

- 2 large bell peppers (any colour), seeded and sliced into strips
- 1 tbsp olive oil
- 1 tsp smoked paprika
- Salt and black pepper, to taste
- For the Cilantro Lime Sauce:
- 100ml Greek yoghurt
- 2 tbsp chopped fresh cilantro
- 1 tbsp lime juice
- 1 clove garlic, minced
- Salt and black pepper, to taste

Preparation instructions:

1. Preheat the Air Fryer to 200°C for 5 minutes.

2. In a bowl, toss the bell pepper strips with olive oil, smoked paprika, salt, and black pepper.

3. Place the bell pepper strips in the Air Fryer basket, ensuring they are in a single layer without overcrowding.

4. Air fry at 200°C for 12-15 minutes until the bell peppers are tender and slightly charred, tossing them halfway through cooking.

5. While the bell peppers are cooking, prepare the cilantro lime sauce. In a separate bowl, combine the Greek yoghurt, chopped fresh cilantro, lime juice, minced garlic, salt, and black pepper. Mix well.

6. Once the bell pepper strips are cooked, remove them from the Air Fryer and let them cool for a few minutes.

7. Serve the smoky paprika roasted bell pepper strips with the cilantro lime sauce on the side.

8. Enjoy the smoky and flavorful bell peppers dipped in the tangy cilantro lime sauce.

Grilled Watermelon Skewers with Feta and Mint

Serves: 4
Prep time: 10 minutes / Cook time: 5 minutes

Ingredients:
- 400g watermelon, cut into cubes
- 100g feta cheese, crumbled
- 2 tbsp chopped fresh mint
- 1 tbsp olive oil
- 1 tsp balsamic glaze (optional)

Preparation instructions:
1. Preheat the Air Fryer to 200°C for 5 minutes.
2. Thread the watermelon cubes onto skewers.
3. Brush the watermelon skewers with olive oil on all sides.
4. Place the skewers in the Air Fryer basket, ensuring they are in a single layer without overcrowding.
5. Air fry at 200°C for 4-5 minutes until the watermelon is slightly charred and caramelised.
6. Once the watermelon skewers are cooked, remove them from the Air Fryer and let them cool for a few minutes.
7. Sprinkle the crumbled feta cheese and chopped fresh mint over the grilled watermelon skewers.
8. Drizzle with balsamic glaze, if desired, for an extra touch of sweetness and tanginess.
9. Serve the grilled watermelon skewers as a unique and refreshing appetiser or side dish.
10. Enjoy the combination of juicy watermelon, creamy feta cheese, and aromatic mint in every bite.

Asian Sesame Cucumber Noodle Salad with Peanut Dressing

Serves: 4
Prep time: 15 minutes / Cook time: 5 minutes

Ingredients:
- 2 large cucumbers, spiralized or thinly sliced
- 50g carrots, julienned
- 50g red bell pepper, thinly sliced
- 50g edamame beans, cooked
- 2 green onions, sliced
- 2 tbsp sesame seeds

For the Peanut Dressing:
- 3 tbsp peanut butter
- 2 tbsp soy sauce
- 1 tbsp rice vinegar
- 1 tbsp sesame oil
- 1 tbsp honey
- 1 clove garlic, minced
- 1 tsp grated fresh ginger
- 2-3 tbsp water (as needed)

Preparation instructions:
1. In a large bowl, combine the cucumber noodles, julienned carrots, sliced red bell pepper, edamame beans, green onions, and sesame seeds.
2. Preheat the Air Fryer to 200°C for 5 minutes.
3. In a separate bowl, whisk together the peanut butter, soy sauce, rice vinegar, sesame oil, honey, minced garlic, grated ginger, and water until well combined. Adjust the consistency with more water if needed.
4. Pour the peanut dressing over the cucumber noodle salad and toss to coat the vegetables evenly.
5. Air fry at 200°C for 4-5 minutes
6. Let the salad sit for a few minutes to allow the flavours to meld together.
7. Serve the Asian sesame cucumber noodle salad as a refreshing and nutritious side dish or light meal.
8. Enjoy the crunchy textures, vibrant colours, and delicious peanut dressing in this flavorful salad.

Lemon Dill Roasted Radishes with Greek Yoghurt Dip

Serves: 4
Prep time: 10 minutes / Cook time: 15 minutes

Ingredients:
- 400g radishes, halved
- 1 tbsp olive oil
- 1 tbsp lemon juice
- 1 tbsp chopped fresh dill
- Salt and black pepper, to taste

For the Greek Yoghurt Dip:
- 150g Greek yoghurt
- 1 tbsp chopped fresh dill
- 1 tbsp lemon juice
- 1 clove garlic, minced
- Salt and black pepper, to taste

Preparation instructions:

1. Preheat the Air Fryer to 200°C for 5 minutes.
2. In a bowl, toss the radish halves with olive oil, lemon juice, chopped fresh dill, salt, and black pepper.
3. Place the radishes in the Air Fryer basket, ensuring they are in a single layer without overcrowding.
4. Air fry at 200°C for 12-15 minutes until the radishes are tender and lightly browned, shaking them halfway through cooking.
5. While the radishes are cooking, prepare the Greek yoghurt dip. In a separate bowl, combine the Greek yoghurt, chopped fresh dill, lemon juice, minced garlic, salt, and black pepper. Mix well.
6. Once the radishes are cooked, remove them from the Air Fryer and let them cool for a few minutes.
7. Serve the lemon dill roasted radishes with the Greek yoghurt dip on the side.
8. Enjoy the zesty and herb-infused radishes paired with the creamy and tangy Greek yoghurt dip.

Roasted Beet and Goat Cheese Salad with Honey Lime Vinaigrette

Serves: 4
Prep time: 15 minutes / Cook time: 35 minutes

Ingredients:

- 500g beets, peeled and cubed
- 2 tbsp olive oil
- Salt and black pepper, to taste
- 100g mixed salad greens
- 100g crumbled goat cheese
- 50g walnuts, toasted
- 2 tbsp chopped fresh parsley

For the Honey Lime Vinaigrette:

- 2 tbsp olive oil
- 1 tbsp lime juice
- 1 tbsp honey
- 1 clove garlic, minced
- Salt and black pepper, to taste

Preparation instructions:

1. Preheat the Air Fryer to 200°C for 5 minutes.
2. In a bowl, toss the beet cubes with olive oil, salt, and black pepper.
3. Place the beets in the Air Fryer basket, ensuring they are in a single layer without overcrowding.
4. Air fry at 200°C for 30-35 minutes until the beets

are tender and slightly caramelised, shaking them halfway through cooking.

5. While the beets are roasting, prepare the honey lime vinaigrette. In a separate bowl, whisk together the olive oil, lime juice, honey, minced garlic, salt, and black pepper until well combined.
6. Once the beets are cooked, remove them from the Air Fryer and let them cool for a few minutes.
7. In a serving bowl, combine the mixed salad greens, roasted beets, crumbled goat cheese, toasted walnuts, and chopped fresh parsley.
8. Drizzle the honey lime vinaigrette over the salad and toss to coat.
9. Serve the roasted beet and goat cheese salad as a vibrant and nutritious main course or side dish.
10. Enjoy the earthy flavours of the roasted beets, creamy goat cheese, and crunchy walnuts with the tangy sweetness of the honey lime vinaigrette.

Spiced Apple Rings with Almond Butter Drizzle

Serves: 4
Prep time: 10 minutes / Cook time: 10 minutes

Ingredients:

- 2 large apples, cored and sliced into rings
- 2 tbsp melted coconut oil
- 1 tbsp honey
- 1 tsp ground cinnamon
- 1/4 tsp ground nutmeg
- 1/4 tsp ground cloves

For the Almond Butter Drizzle:

- 4 tbsp almond butter
- 2 tbsp maple syrup
- 2 tbsp warm water

Preparation instructions:

1. Preheat the Air Fryer to 180°C for 5 minutes.
2. In a bowl, combine the melted coconut oil, honey, ground cinnamon, ground nutmeg, and ground cloves.
3. Dip each apple ring into the spiced mixture, ensuring they are evenly coated.
4. Place the coated apple rings in the Air Fryer basket, ensuring they are in a single layer without overlapping.
5. Air fry at 180°C for 8-10 minutes until the apple rings are tender and slightly caramelised.

6. While the apple rings are cooking, prepare the almond butter drizzle. In a separate bowl, whisk together the almond butter, maple syrup, and warm water until smooth and pourable.
7. Once the apple rings are cooked, remove them from the Air Fryer and let them cool for a few minutes.
8. Drizzle the almond butter mixture over the spiced apple rings.
9. Serve the spiced apple rings with almond butter drizzle as a delicious and healthier dessert or snack option.
10. Enjoy the warm and fragrant flavours of the spiced apples paired with the creamy and nutty almond butter drizzle.

Roasted Portobello Mushroom Cap "Burger" with Avocado and Tomato

Serves: 4
Prep time: 15 minutes / Cook time: 15 minutes

Ingredients:
- 4 large portobello mushroom caps
- 2 tbsp balsamic vinegar
- 2 tbsp olive oil
- 2 cloves garlic, minced
- 1 tsp dried thyme
- Salt and black pepper, to taste
- 4 burger buns
- 1 ripe avocado, sliced
- 1 large tomato, sliced
- Mixed salad greens, for serving

Preparation instructions:
1. Preheat the Air Fryer to 200°C for 5 minutes.
2. In a bowl, whisk together the balsamic vinegar, olive oil, minced garlic, dried thyme, salt, and black pepper.
3. Place the portobello mushroom caps in a shallow dish and pour the marinade over them. Let them marinate for 10 minutes, turning occasionally.
4. Remove the mushroom caps from the marinade, reserving the marinade for later use.
5. Place the mushroom caps in the Air Fryer basket, gill side up.
6. Air fry at 200°C for 12-15 minutes until the mushroom caps are tender and juicy, basting them with the

reserved marinade halfway through cooking.
7. While the mushroom caps are cooking, toast the burger buns if desired.
8. Once the mushroom caps are cooked, remove them from the Air Fryer and let them cool for a few minutes.
9. Assemble the "burgers" by placing a portobello mushroom cap on the bottom half of each burger bun.
10. Top with avocado slices, tomato slices, and mixed salad greens.
11. Place the top half of the burger buns on each assembled "burger."
12. Serve the roasted portobello mushroom cap "burgers" as a satisfying and flavorful vegetarian meal option.
13. Enjoy the meaty texture and rich flavour of the roasted portobello mushrooms combined with the creamy avocado and fresh tomato.

Honey Lime Glazed Grilled Pineapple Rings with Coconut Whipped Cream

Serves: 4
Prep time: 10 minutes / Cook time: 6 minutes

Ingredients:
- 1 large pineapple, peeled and sliced into rings
- 2 tbsp honey
- 2 tbsp lime juice
- 1/2 tsp ground cinnamon
- 1/4 tsp ground ginger
- 1/4 tsp ground nutmeg
- 200ml coconut cream
- 1 tbsp powdered sugar
- 1/2 tsp vanilla extract
- Toasted coconut flakes, for garnish (optional)

Preparation instructions:
1. Preheat the Air Fryer to 200°C for 5 minutes.
2. In a bowl, whisk together the honey, lime juice, ground cinnamon, ground ginger, and ground nutmeg.
3. Brush the pineapple rings with the honey lime glaze on both sides.
4. Place the pineapple rings in the Air Fryer basket, ensuring they are in a single layer without overcrowding.

5. Air fry at 200°C for 3 minutes on each side until the pineapple rings are caramelised and slightly charred.

6. While the pineapple rings are cooking, prepare the coconut whipped cream. In a chilled mixing bowl, combine the coconut cream, powdered sugar, and vanilla extract. Using an electric mixer, whip the mixture until it reaches a light and fluffy consistency.

7. Once the pineapple rings are cooked, remove them from the Air Fryer and let them cool for a few minutes.

8. Serve the honey lime glazed grilled pineapple rings with a dollop of coconut whipped cream.

9. Sprinkle with toasted coconut flakes for added texture and tropical flavour, if desired.

10. Enjoy the sweet and tangy glaze on the grilled pineapple rings, paired with the creamy and luscious coconut whipped cream.

Roasted Asparagus Spears with Lemon Garlic Aioli

Serves: 4
Prep time: 10 minutes / Cook time: 8 minutes

Ingredients:
- 400g asparagus spears, trimmed
- 2 tbsp olive oil
- Salt and black pepper, to taste
- For the Lemon Garlic Aioli:
- 100g mayonnaise
- 1 clove garlic, minced
- 1 tbsp lemon juice
- 1 tsp grated lemon zest
- Salt and black pepper, to taste

Preparation instructions:
1. Preheat the Air Fryer to 200°C for 5 minutes.
2. In a bowl, toss the asparagus spears with olive oil, salt, and black pepper.
3. Place the asparagus spears in the Air Fryer basket, ensuring they are in a single layer without overcrowding.
4. Air fry at 200°C for 7-8 minutes until the asparagus is tender and lightly charred, shaking them halfway through cooking.
5. While the asparagus is cooking, prepare the lemon garlic aioli. In a separate bowl, whisk together the mayonnaise, minced garlic, lemon juice, grated lemon zest, salt, and black pepper until well combined.

6. Once the asparagus is cooked, remove them from the Air Fryer and let them cool for a few minutes.

7. Serve the roasted asparagus spears with the lemon garlic aioli on the side.

8. Dip the roasted asparagus spears into the flavorful aioli for an extra burst of tangy and garlicky goodness.

9. Enjoy the tender and roasted asparagus with the zesty and creamy lemon garlic aioli as a delicious and nutritious side dish.

Roasted Brussels Sprouts

Serves: 2 people
Prep time: 10 minutes | Cook time: 18 minutes

Ingredients
- 400g Brussels sprouts, halved
- 30 ml olive oil
- 5g garlic powder
- Salt and pepper to taste

Preparation instructions:
1. Preheat the air fryer to 200°C (400°F).
2. In a bowl, toss the halved Brussels sprouts with olive oil, garlic powder, salt, and pepper.
3. Place the Brussels sprouts in a single layer in the air fryer basket.
4. Air fry for 15-18 minutes, shaking the basket occasionally, until the Brussels sprouts are crispy and browned.
5. Remove from the air fryer and serve hot.

Zucchini Fritters

Serves: 4 people
Prep time: 10 minutes | Cook time: 12 minutes

Ingredients:
- 300g zucchini, grated and squeezed dry
- 50g bread crumbs
- 1 egg, beaten
- 15 ml olive oil
- Salt and pepper to taste

Preparation instructions:
1. Preheat the air fryer to 200°C (400°F).
2. In a bowl, combine the grated zucchini, bread crumbs, beaten egg, olive oil, salt, and pepper.
3. Form the mixture into small patties or fritters.

4. Place the zucchini fritters in a single layer in the air fryer basket.
5. Air fry for 10-12 minutes, flipping them halfway through, until the fritters are golden brown and crisp.
6. Remove them from the air fryer and let them cool slightly before serving.

Cinnamon Apple Chips

Serves: 2 people
Prep time: 10 minutes | Cook time: 1-2 hours

Ingredients:
- 2 apples, thinly sliced
- 5g ground cinnamon
- 15 ml lemon juice

Preparation instructions:
1. Preheat the air fryer to 120°C (250°F).
2. In a bowl, toss the apple slices with ground cinnamon and lemon juice until evenly coated.
3. Place the apple slices in a single layer in the air fryer basket.
4. Air fry for 1-2 hours, flipping them occasionally, until the apple chips are dry and crispy.
5. Remove from the air fryer and let them cool completely before enjoying.

Parmesan Zucchini Fries

Serves: 2 people
Prep time: 20 minutes | Cook time: 12 minutes

Ingredients:
- 2 zucchini, cut into fry-shaped sticks
- 50g grated Parmesan cheese
- 50g bread crumbs
- 1 teaspoon Italian seasoning
- Salt and pepper to taste
- 1 egg, beaten

Preparation instructions:
1. Preheat the air fryer to 200°C (400°F).
2. In a shallow bowl, mix together the Parmesan cheese, bread crumbs, Italian seasoning, salt, and pepper.
3. Dip each zucchini stick into the beaten egg, allowing the excess to drip off.
4. Roll the zucchini stick in the Parmesan mixture, pressing gently to adhere.
5. Place the coated zucchini sticks in a single layer

in the air fryer basket.
6. Air fry for 10-12 minutes, flipping them halfway through, until the fries are golden and crispy.
7. Remove from the air fryer and serve hot with your favourite dipping sauce.

Honey-Glazed Carrots

Serves: 2-4 people
Prep time: 10 minutes | Cook time: 15 minutes

Ingredients:
- 500g baby carrots
- 30 ml olive oil
- 30 ml honey
- 5g ground cumin
- Salt and pepper to taste
- Fresh parsley for garnish (optional)

Preparation instructions:
1. Preheat the air fryer to 200°C (400°F).
2. In a bowl, toss the baby carrots with olive oil, honey, ground cumin, salt, and pepper until well-coated.
3. Place the coated carrots in a single layer in the air fryer basket.
4. Air fry for 12-15 minutes, shaking the basket occasionally, until the carrots are tender and caramelised.
5. Remove from the air fryer and garnish with fresh parsley if desired.
6. Serve hot as a delightful side dish to your favourite meals.

Garlic-Parmesan Broccoli

Serves: 2-4 people
Prep time: 10 minutes | Cook time: 15-18 minutes

Ingredients:
- 500g broccoli florets
- 30 ml olive oil
- 5g garlic powder
- 50g grated Parmesan cheese
- Salt and pepper to taste
- Lemon wedges for serving

Preparation instructions:
1. Preheat the air fryer to 200°C (400°F).
2. In a bowl, toss the broccoli florets with olive oil, garlic powder, salt, and pepper until well-coated.
3. Place the coated broccoli florets in a single layer in the air fryer basket.
4. Air fry for 12-15 minutes, shaking the basket

occasionally, until the broccoli is tender and lightly browned.

5. Sprinkle the grated Parmesan cheese over the broccoli and air fry for an additional 2-3 minutes until the cheese is melted and crispy.
6. Remove from the air fryer and serve hot with lemon wedges for a zesty touch.

Cinnamon-Roasted Butternut Squash

Serves: 2-4 people
Prep time: 15 minutes | Cook time: 12-15 minutes

Ingredients:

- 500g butternut squash, peeled and cubed
- 30 ml olive oil
- 5g ground cinnamon
- 15g brown sugar (optional, for added sweetness)
- Salt and pepper to taste

Preparation instructions:

1. Preheat the air fryer to 200°C (400°F).
2. In a bowl, toss the butternut squash cubes with olive oil, ground cinnamon, brown sugar (if using), salt, and pepper until well-coated.
3. Place the coated squash cubes in a single layer in the air fryer basket.
4. Air fry for 12-15 minutes, shaking the basket occasionally, until the squash is tender and caramelised.
5. Remove from the air fryer and serve hot as a delightful side dish or a tasty addition to salads and grain bowls.

Stuffed Bell Peppers

Serves: 2 people
Prep time: 20-30 minutes | Cook time: 20-25 minutes

Ingredients:

- 4 bell peppers (any colour), tops removed and seeds removed
- 200g cooked quinoa
- 150g diced tomatoes
- 100g black beans, rinsed and drained
- 50g corn kernels
- 50g shredded cheese (such as cheddar or mozzarella)
- 5g chilli powder
- 5g ground cumin

- Salt and pepper to taste

Preparation instructions:

1. Preheat the air fryer to 180°C (350°F).
2. In a bowl, combine the cooked quinoa, diced tomatoes, black beans, corn kernels, shredded cheese, chilli powder, ground cumin, salt, and pepper. Mix well to combine.
3. Stuff each bell pepper with the quinoa filling, pressing gently to fill them completely.
4. Place the stuffed bell peppers in the air fryer basket.
5. Air fry for 20-25 minutes, until the peppers are tender and the filling is heated through.
6. Remove from the air fryer and let them cool slightly before serving.

Buffalo Cauliflower Wings

Serves: 2 people
Prep time: 15-20 minutes | Cook time: 15-18 minutes

Ingredients:

- 1 medium head of cauliflower, cut into florets
- 60g all-purpose flour
- 5g garlic powder
- 5g paprika
- 5g salt
- 120 ml milk (or plant-based milk for vegan option)
- 60 ml hot sauce
- 30g unsalted butter (or plant-based butter for vegan option)

Preparation instructions:

1. Preheat the air fryer to 200°C (400°F).
2. In a bowl, combine the all-purpose flour, garlic powder, paprika, and salt. Mix well.
3. Dip each cauliflower floret into the milk, allowing any excess to drip off.
4. Coat the cauliflower floret in the flour mixture, pressing lightly to adhere.
5. Place the coated cauliflower florets in the air fryer basket, leaving space between them.
6. Air fry for 15-18 minutes, shaking the basket halfway through, until the cauliflower is tender and the coating is crispy and golden.
7. In a small saucepan, melt the butter over low heat. Add the hot sauce and stir until well combined.
8. Once the cauliflower wings are cooked, transfer them to a bowl and pour the buffalo sauce over

them. Toss to coat evenly.

9. Remove the Buffalo Cauliflower Wings from the bowl and let them cool for a few minutes.

10. Serve the cauliflower wings hot with your favourite dipping sauce.

Mediterranean Stuffed Eggplant

Serves: 2-4 people
Prep time: 15-20 minutes | Cook time: 20-25 minutes

Ingredients:

- 2 eggplants
- 150g cooked quinoa
- 100g diced tomatoes
- 100g crumbled feta cheese
- 50g black olives, sliced
- 30 ml olive oil
- 5g dried oregano
- Salt and pepper to taste
- Fresh parsley for garnish (optional)

Preparation instructions:

1. Preheat the air fryer to 200°C (400°F).
2. Cut the eggplants in half lengthwise. Score the flesh in a crisscross pattern, being careful not to pierce the skin.
3. In a bowl, combine the cooked quinoa, diced tomatoes, crumbled feta cheese, black olives, olive oil, dried oregano, salt, and pepper. Mix well.
4. Spoon the quinoa mixture into the hollowed-out eggplants, pressing gently to fill them completely.
5. Place the stuffed eggplants in the air fryer basket.
6. Air fry for 20-25 minutes, until the eggplants are tender and the filling is heated through.
7. Remove from the air fryer and garnish with fresh parsley, if desired, before serving.

Air Fryer Hummus-Stuffed Mushrooms

Serves: 4-6 people
Prep time: 10 minutes | Cook time: 8-10 minutes

Ingredients:

- 8-10 medium-sized button mushrooms
- 120g hummus (store-bought or homemade)
- 15 ml olive oil
- 5g dried oregano
- Salt and pepper to taste
- Fresh parsley (for garnish)

Preparation instructions:

1. Remove the stems from the mushrooms and set them aside.
2. In a small bowl, mix the hummus with olive oil, dried oregano, salt, and pepper.
3. Stuff each mushroom cap with a generous amount of the hummus mixture, ensuring they are filled to the top.
4. Place the mushroom caps and the reserved stems in the air fryer basket.
5. Preheat the air fryer to 180°C (350°F).
6. Air fry for 8-10 minutes until the mushrooms are tender and the filling is heated through.
7. Once cooked, remove the mushrooms from the air fryer and let them cool for a few minutes.
8. Garnish with fresh parsley before serving.
9. Serve the Air Fryer Hummus-Stuffed Mushrooms as a tasty appetiser or finger food. They are best enjoyed warmly.

Garlic Parmesan Roasted Broccoli

Serves: 2-4 people
Prep time: 5-10 minutes | Cook time: 10-12 minutes

Ingredients:

- 500g broccoli florets
- 30 ml olive oil
- 3 cloves garlic, minced
- 30g grated Parmesan cheese
- Salt and pepper to taste

Preparation instructions:

1. Preheat the air fryer to 200°C (400°F).
2. In a large bowl, toss the broccoli florets with olive oil, minced garlic, grated Parmesan cheese, salt, and pepper. Ensure that the broccoli is evenly coated with the mixture.
3. Place the seasoned broccoli florets in the air fryer basket in a single layer.
4. Air fry for 10-12 minutes, shaking the basket halfway through, until the broccoli is tender and lightly browned.
5. Remove the roasted broccoli from the air fryer and transfer it to a serving dish.
6. Serve the Garlic Parmesan Roasted Broccoli as a flavorful and nutritious side dish.

Crunchy Chicken Parmesan Nuggets with Marinara Dipping Sauce

Serves: 4
Prep time: 15 minutes / Cook time: 12 minutes

Ingredients:

For the Chicken Parmesan Nuggets:
- 400g boneless, skinless chicken breasts, cut into bite-sized pieces
- 100g breadcrumbs
- 50g grated Parmesan cheese
- 1 tsp dried oregano
- 1 tsp dried basil
- 1/2 tsp garlic powder
- 1/2 tsp onion powder
- 1/4 tsp paprika
- Salt and black pepper, to taste
- 2 large eggs, beaten
- 60ml milk

For the Marinara Dipping Sauce:
- 200g tomato passata
- 1 clove garlic, minced
- 1 tsp dried basil
- 1 tsp dried oregano
- 1/2 tsp sugar
- Salt and black pepper, to taste

Preparation instructions:

1. Preheat the Air Fryer to 200°C for 5 minutes.
2. In a shallow bowl, combine the breadcrumbs, grated Parmesan cheese, dried oregano, dried basil, garlic powder, onion powder, paprika, salt, and black pepper. Mix well.
3. In a separate bowl, whisk together the eggs and milk.
4. Dip each chicken piece into the egg mixture, allowing any excess to drip off, then coat it with the breadcrumb mixture, pressing gently to adhere. Repeat with all the chicken pieces.
5. Place the coated chicken nuggets in the Air Fryer basket, ensuring they are in a single layer without overcrowding.
6. Air fry at 200°C for 10-12 minutes, flipping halfway through cooking, until the chicken nuggets are golden brown and cooked through.
7. While the chicken is cooking, prepare the marinara dipping sauce. In a small saucepan, combine the tomato passata, minced garlic, dried basil, dried oregano, sugar, salt, and black pepper. Heat over medium heat until warmed through.
8. Once the chicken nuggets are cooked, remove them from the Air Fryer and let them cool for a few minutes.
9. Serve the crunchy chicken Parmesan nuggets with the marinara dipping sauce on the side.
10. Dip the nuggets into the tangy and flavorful marinara sauce for a delicious and satisfying snack or meal.
11. Enjoy the crispy and cheesy chicken Parmesan nuggets with the homemade marinara sauce for a taste of Italy in every bite.

Cheesy Beef and Veggie Stuffed Bell Peppers

Serves: 4
Prep time: 15 minutes / Cook time: 20 minutes

Ingredients:
- 4 bell peppers (any colour), tops removed and seeds removed
- 300g ground beef
- 1 small onion, diced
- 1 small zucchini, diced
- 1 small red bell pepper, diced
- 1 small carrot, grated
- 2 cloves garlic, minced
- 200g cooked rice
- 200g grated cheddar cheese
- 1 tsp dried oregano
- 1 tsp dried basil
- 1/2 tsp paprika
- Salt and black pepper, to taste
- 2 tbsp olive oil

Preparation instructions:
1. Preheat the Air Fryer to 190°C for 5 minutes.
2. In a large skillet, heat olive oil over medium heat. Add the ground beef and cook until browned.

Remove the excess fat.

3. Add the diced onion, zucchini, red bell pepper, grated carrot, and minced garlic to the skillet. Sauté until the vegetables are tender.

4. Stir in the cooked rice, dried oregano, dried basil, paprika, salt, and black pepper. Cook for an additional 2-3 minutes to combine the flavours.

5. Stuff each bell pepper with the beef and vegetable mixture. Place them in the crisper basket of the Air Fryer.

6. Air fry at 190°C for 18-20 minutes or until the bell peppers are tender and the filling is heated through.

7. Sprinkle the grated cheddar cheese evenly over the stuffed bell peppers.

8. Air fry for an additional 2-3 minutes or until the cheese is melted and bubbly.

9. Carefully remove the stuffed bell peppers from the Air Fryer and let them cool for a few minutes before serving.

10. Enjoy these delicious and cheesy beef and veggie stuffed bell peppers as a satisfying and nutritious meal.

Tex-Mex Loaded Sweet Potato Skins with Guacamole

Serves: 4
Prep time: 15 minutes / Cook time: 30 minutes

Ingredients:
- 4 medium sweet potatoes
- 200g cooked black beans
- 200g sweetcorn kernels
- 1 small red onion, finely diced
- 1 small red bell pepper, finely diced
- 1 small jalapeño pepper, seeds removed and finely diced
- 2 tbsp chopped fresh cilantro
- 1 tsp ground cumin
- 1 tsp chilli powder
- 1/2 tsp paprika
- 1/4 tsp garlic powder
- Salt and black pepper, to taste
- 150g grated cheddar cheese
- Guacamole, for serving

Preparation instructions:
1. Preheat the Air Fryer to 190°C for 5 minutes.
2. Wash the sweet potatoes and pat them dry. Pierce each sweet potato several times with a fork to allow steam to escape during cooking.

3. Place the sweet potatoes in the Air Fryer basket and air fry at 190°C for 25-30 minutes or until the sweet potatoes are tender.

4. While the sweet potatoes are cooking, prepare the filling. In a bowl, combine the cooked black beans, sweetcorn kernels, diced red onion, diced red bell pepper, diced jalapeño pepper, chopped cilantro, ground cumin, chilli powder, paprika, garlic powder, salt, and black pepper. Mix well to combine.

5. Once the sweet potatoes are cooked, remove them from the Air Fryer and let them cool slightly.

6. Cut each sweet potato in half lengthwise. Scoop out the flesh, leaving a thin layer attached to the skin. Reserve the sweet potato flesh for another use.

7. Fill each sweet potato skin with the Tex-Mex filling mixture. Sprinkle grated cheddar cheese over the top of each filled sweet potato skin.

8. Return the sweet potato skins to the Air Fryer basket and air fry at 190°C for 5-7 minutes or until the cheese is melted and bubbly.

9. Remove the loaded sweet potato skins from the Air Fryer and serve them hot with a side of guacamole.

10. Enjoy these delicious Tex-Mex loaded sweet potato skins as a flavorful and satisfying appetiser or main dish.

Hawaiian BBQ Chicken Sliders with Pineapple Salsa

Serves: 4
Prep time: 15 minutes / Cook time: 15 minutes

Ingredients:
- 300g boneless, skinless chicken breasts
- 120ml barbecue sauce
- 4 small burger buns
- 4 pineapple rings
- 1 small red onion, thinly sliced
- 4 leaves lettuce
- Salt and black pepper, to taste

Pineapple Salsa:
- 200g fresh pineapple, finely diced
- 1/4 red bell pepper, finely diced
- 1/4 red onion, finely diced
- 2 tbsp chopped fresh cilantro

- Juice of 1 lime
- Salt and black pepper, to taste

Preparation instructions:
1. Preheat the Air Fryer to 190°C for 5 minutes.
2. Season the chicken breasts with salt and black pepper. Brush both sides of the chicken breasts with barbecue sauce.
3. Place the chicken breasts in the Air Fryer basket and air fry at 190°C for 12-15 minutes or until the chicken is cooked through and reaches an internal temperature of 75°C.
4. While the chicken is cooking, prepare the pineapple salsa. In a bowl, combine the diced pineapple, diced red bell pepper, diced red onion, chopped cilantro, lime juice, salt, and black pepper. Mix well to combine.
5. Remove the cooked chicken from the Air Fryer and let it rest for a few minutes. Then, shred the chicken using two forks.
6. Toast the burger buns in the Air Fryer for 1-2 minutes until slightly crispy.
7. Assemble the sliders by placing a lettuce leaf on the bottom half of each toasted bun. Top with a generous amount of shredded BBQ chicken, a pineapple ring, a few slices of red onion, and a spoonful of pineapple salsa. Cover with the top half of the bun.
8. Serve the Hawaiian BBQ chicken sliders with pineapple salsa as a delicious and tropical meal or party appetiser.
9. Enjoy!

Crispy Ranch Seasoned Fish Tacos with Lime Crema

Serves: 4
Prep time: 15 minutes / Cook time: 10 minutes

Ingredients:
- 400g white fish fillets (such as cod or haddock)
- 60g all-purpose flour
- 2 tbsp ranch seasoning mix
- 1/4 tsp garlic powder
- 1/4 tsp paprika
- Salt and black pepper, to taste
- 2 large eggs, beaten
- 80g breadcrumbs
- 8 small flour tortillas

- Shredded lettuce, for serving
- Diced tomatoes, for serving
- Chopped fresh cilantro, for serving
- Lime wedges, for serving
- Lime Crema:
- 120ml sour cream
- Juice of 1 lime
- 1/4 tsp garlic powder
- Salt and black pepper, to taste

Preparation instructions:
1. Preheat the Air Fryer to 190°C for 5 minutes.
2. Cut the fish fillets into small, manageable pieces.
3. In a shallow dish, combine the flour, ranch seasoning mix, garlic powder, paprika, salt, and black pepper.
4. Place the beaten eggs in a separate shallow dish.
5. Dip each piece of fish into the flour mixture, then into the beaten eggs, and finally coat it with breadcrumbs, pressing gently to adhere.
6. Place the breaded fish pieces in the Air Fryer basket, ensuring they are not overcrowded.
7. Air fry at 190°C for 8-10 minutes or until the fish is crispy and cooked through.
8. While the fish is cooking, prepare the lime crema. In a small bowl, whisk together the sour cream, lime juice, garlic powder, salt, and black pepper. Adjust the seasoning to taste.
9. Warm the flour tortillas in the Air Fryer for 1-2 minutes.
10. Assemble the fish tacos by placing a piece of crispy fish on each warmed tortilla. Top with shredded lettuce, diced tomatoes, chopped cilantro, and a dollop of lime crema. Squeeze fresh lime juice over the top.
11. Serve the crispy ranch seasoned fish tacos with lime crema as a delightful and flavorful meal.
12. Enjoy!

Teriyaki Glazed Meatball Skewers with Vegetable Fried Rice

Serves: 4
Prep time: 20 minutes / Cook time: 25 minutes

Ingredients:
For the meatballs:
- 500g ground beef
- 60g breadcrumbs

- 60g finely chopped onion
- 1 clove garlic, minced
- 2 tbsp soy sauce
- 1 tbsp brown sugar
- 1/2 tsp ground ginger
- 1/4 tsp black pepper
- 1/4 tsp sesame oil
- 1 egg, beaten

For the teriyaki glaze:
- 60ml soy sauce
- 60ml water
- 2 tbsp brown sugar
- 1 tbsp honey
- 1 tbsp rice vinegar
- 1 clove garlic, minced
- 1/2 tsp ground ginger
- 1 tsp cornstarch

For the vegetable fried rice:
- 200g cooked rice
- 150g mixed vegetables (carrots, peas, corn)
- 1 small onion, diced
- 2 cloves garlic, minced
- 2 tbsp soy sauce
- 1 tbsp sesame oil
- 2 eggs, beaten
- Salt and black pepper, to taste
- 2 spring onions, sliced (for garnish)

For the skewers:
- 8 wooden skewers, soaked in water for 20 minutes

Preparation instructions:

1. Preheat the Air Fryer to 190°C for 5 minutes.
2. In a large bowl, combine the ground beef, breadcrumbs, finely chopped onion, minced garlic, soy sauce, brown sugar, ground ginger, black pepper, sesame oil, and beaten egg. Mix well until all the Ingredients are evenly incorporated.
3. Shape the meat mixture into small meatballs, about 2-3 cm in diameter.
4. Place the meatballs in the Air Fryer basket, ensuring they are not touching.
5. Air fry at 190°C for 12-15 minutes or until the meatballs are cooked through and browned.
6. While the meatballs are cooking, prepare the teriyaki glaze. In a small saucepan, combine the soy sauce, water, brown sugar, honey, rice vinegar, minced garlic, and ground ginger. Bring

the mixture to a simmer over medium heat. In a separate bowl, dissolve the cornstarch in a small amount of water to make a slurry. Add the slurry to the simmering sauce, stirring constantly until the sauce thickens. Remove from heat and set aside.

7. In a large skillet or wok, heat the sesame oil over medium heat. Add the diced onion and minced garlic, and sauté until the onion becomes translucent.
8. Add the mixed vegetables to the skillet and stir-fry for a few minutes until they are slightly tender.
9. Push the vegetables to one side of the skillet and add the beaten eggs to the other side. Scramble the eggs until cooked, then mix them together with the vegetables.
10. Add the cooked rice to the skillet and pour the soy sauce over the top. Stir-fry everything together, coating the rice and vegetables with the sauce. Cook for an additional 3-4 minutes until the fried rice is heated through. Season with salt and black pepper to taste.
11. Thread the cooked meatballs onto the soaked wooden skewers.
12. Brush the teriyaki glaze over the meatball skewers, coating them evenly.
13. Place the skewers in the Air Fryer basket and air fry at 190°C for 3-4 minutes to glaze the meatballs.
14. Serve the teriyaki glazed meatball skewers with vegetable fried rice. Garnish with sliced spring onions.
15. Enjoy this delicious and satisfying Asian-inspired meal!

Spinach and Ricotta Stuffed Shells with Marinara Sauce

Serves: 4
Prep time: 20 minutes / Cook time: 20 minutes

Ingredients:
- 250g jumbo pasta shells
- 200g fresh spinach, chopped
- 250g ricotta cheese
- 100g grated Parmesan cheese
- 1 large egg
- 1/4 tsp garlic powder
- 1/4 tsp onion powder

- Salt and black pepper, to taste
- 500ml marinara sauce
- Fresh basil leaves, for garnish

Preparation instructions:

1. Preheat the Air Fryer to 190°C for 5 minutes.
2. Cook the jumbo pasta shells according to the package instructions until al dente. Drain and set aside.
3. In a large bowl, combine the chopped spinach, ricotta cheese, grated Parmesan cheese, egg, garlic powder, onion powder, salt, and black pepper. Mix well until all the Ingredients are evenly incorporated.
4. Stuff each cooked pasta shell with a generous amount of the spinach and ricotta mixture.
5. Place the stuffed shells in the crisper basket of the Air Fryer, ensuring they are not overcrowded.
6. Air fry at 190°C for 15-18 minutes or until the shells are heated through and the cheese is melted and slightly golden.
7. While the shells are cooking, warm the marinara sauce in a saucepan over medium heat.
8. Serve the spinach and ricotta stuffed shells with marinara sauce. Garnish with fresh basil leaves.
9. Enjoy this delicious and comforting Italian-inspired dish!

BBQ Pulled Pork Loaded Nachos with Avocado Lime Crema

Serves: 4
Prep time: 15 minutes / Cook time: 20 minutes

Ingredients:

- 400g pulled pork
- 200g tortilla chips
- 150g shredded cheddar cheese
- 100g diced red onion
- 100g diced tomatoes
- 50g sliced jalapeños
- 50g chopped fresh cilantro
- 60ml BBQ sauce
- 60ml sour cream
- 1 ripe avocado
- Juice of 1 lime
- Salt and black pepper, to taste

Preparation instructions:

1. Preheat the Air Fryer to 190°C for 5 minutes.

2. In a medium bowl, toss the pulled pork with the BBQ sauce until evenly coated.
3. Spread a layer of tortilla chips on the bottom of the Air Fryer basket.
4. Top the chips with half of the pulled pork, shredded cheddar cheese, diced red onion, and diced tomatoes.
5. Repeat with another layer of chips and the remaining Ingredients.
6. Air fry at 190°C for 8-10 minutes or until the cheese is melted and bubbly.
7. While the nachos are cooking, prepare the avocado lime crema. In a blender or food processor, combine the ripe avocado, sour cream, lime juice, salt, and black pepper. Blend until smooth and creamy.
8. Once the nachos are cooked, remove them from the Air Fryer and drizzle with the avocado lime crema.
9. Garnish with sliced jalapeños and chopped fresh cilantro.
10. Serve the BBQ pulled pork loaded nachos as a delicious and indulgent appetiser or meal.
11. Enjoy!

Caprese Stuffed Chicken Breast with Balsamic Glaze

Serves: 4
Prep time: 15 minutes / Cook time: 25 minutes

Ingredients:

- 4 boneless, skinless chicken breasts
- 150g fresh mozzarella cheese, sliced
- 4 large basil leaves
- 2 large tomatoes, sliced
- 2 tbsp balsamic glaze
- 2 tbsp olive oil
- Salt and black pepper, to taste

Preparation instructions:

1. Preheat the Air Fryer to 190°C for 5 minutes.
2. Make a horizontal cut in each chicken breast to create a pocket for stuffing.
3. Season the inside of each chicken breast with salt and black pepper.
4. Stuff each chicken breast with mozzarella cheese, a basil leaf, and tomato slices.
5. Secure the openings with toothpicks to keep the

stuffing in place.

6. Brush the chicken breasts with olive oil and season with salt and black pepper.

7. Place the chicken breasts in the Air Fryer basket.

8. Air fry at 190°C for 20-25 minutes or until the chicken is cooked through and the cheese is melted and slightly browned.

9. Once cooked, drizzle the chicken breasts with balsamic glaze.

10. Serve the caprese stuffed chicken breasts as a delicious and elegant main course.

11. Enjoy this flavorful and satisfying dish!

Mexican Street Corn Chicken Quesadillas with Lime Crema

Serves: 4
Prep time: 15 minutes / Cook time: 20 minutes

Ingredients:
- 4 large flour tortillas
- 2 cooked chicken breasts, shredded
- 200g Mexican street corn (corn kernels, mayonnaise, Cotija cheese, chilli powder, lime juice, cilantro)
- 150g shredded Monterey Jack cheese
- 60ml sour cream
- Juice of 1 lime
- Salt and black pepper, to taste
- Fresh cilantro leaves, for garnish

Preparation instructions:
1. Preheat the Air Fryer to 190°C for 5 minutes.
2. In a bowl, combine the shredded chicken with the Mexican street corn. Mix well to coat the chicken with the flavours of the corn mixture.
3. In a separate bowl, combine the sour cream, lime juice, salt, and black pepper to make the lime crema. Set aside.
4. Place a flour tortilla on a clean surface and spread a layer of the chicken and corn mixture over half of the tortilla.
5. Sprinkle shredded Monterey Jack cheese over the chicken mixture.
6. Fold the tortilla in half to cover the filling and press lightly to seal.
7. Repeat with the remaining tortillas and filling.
8. Place the quesadillas in the Air Fryer basket, ensuring they are not overlapping.

9. Air fry at 190°C for 8-10 minutes or until the tortillas are crispy and the cheese is melted.

10. While the quesadillas are cooking, prepare the lime crema by mixing the sour cream, lime juice, salt, and black pepper.

11. Once cooked, remove the quesadillas from the Air Fryer and let them cool for a minute or two.

12. Cut the quesadillas into wedges and serve with lime crema.

13. Garnish with fresh cilantro leaves.

14. Enjoy these delicious Mexican street corn chicken quesadillas as a flavorful and satisfying meal!

Philly Cheesesteak Stuffed Peppers with Provolone Cheese

Serves: 4
Prep time: 20 minutes / Cook time: 20 minutes

Ingredients:
- 4 large bell peppers (any colour), halved and seeds removed
- 400g ribeye steak, thinly sliced
- 1 large onion, thinly sliced
- 200g sliced mushrooms
- 200g provolone cheese, sliced
- 2 tbsp olive oil
- Salt and black pepper, to taste

Preparation instructions:
1. Preheat the Air Fryer to 190°C for 5 minutes.
2. In a large skillet, heat the olive oil over medium heat.
3. Add the sliced onions and mushrooms to the skillet and sauté until they are softened and lightly browned.
4. Push the onions and mushrooms to one side of the skillet and add the sliced ribeye steak to the other side.
5. Season the steak with salt and black pepper and cook until it is browned and cooked to your desired doneness.
6. Mix the onions, mushrooms, and steak together in the skillet.
7. Stuff each bell pepper half with the steak and vegetable mixture.
8. Top each stuffed pepper with provolone cheese slices.
9. Place the stuffed peppers in the Air Fryer basket.

10. Air fry at 190°C for 15-20 minutes or until the peppers are tender and the cheese is melted and bubbly.
11. Once cooked, remove the stuffed peppers from the Air Fryer and let them cool for a few minutes.
12. Serve the Philly cheesesteak stuffed peppers as a delicious and hearty meal.
13. Enjoy this tasty twist on a classic Philly favourite!

Pesto Turkey Meatball Subs with Mozzarella Cheese

Serves: 4
Prep time: 15 minutes / Cook time: 15 minutes

Ingredients:
For the turkey meatballs:
- 500g ground turkey
- 60g breadcrumbs
- 1 large egg
- 30g grated Parmesan cheese
- 2 tbsp pesto sauce
- 2 cloves garlic, minced
- 1/4 tsp dried oregano
- Salt and black pepper, to taste

For the subs:
- 4 sub rolls
- 120g mozzarella cheese, sliced
- 120ml marinara sauce
- Fresh basil leaves, for garnish

Preparation instructions:
1. Preheat the Air Fryer to 190°C for 5 minutes.
2. In a bowl, combine the ground turkey, breadcrumbs, egg, Parmesan cheese, pesto sauce, minced garlic, dried oregano, salt, and black pepper. Mix well to combine.
3. Shape the mixture into small meatballs, about 2-3 cm in diameter.
4. Place the meatballs in the Air Fryer basket, ensuring they are not overcrowded.
5. Air fry at 190°C for 12-15 minutes or until the meatballs are cooked through and browned.
6. While the meatballs are cooking, slice the sub rolls lengthwise and place them in the Air Fryer basket to toast for 2-3 minutes until they are lightly crispy.
7. Once the meatballs and sub rolls are cooked, assemble the subs by placing several meatballs on each roll.

8. Top the meatballs with marinara sauce and slices of mozzarella cheese.
9. Place the subs back in the Air Fryer and air fry at 190°C for 3-4 minutes or until the cheese is melted and bubbly.
10. Garnish with fresh basil leaves.
11. Serve the pesto turkey meatball subs as a delicious and satisfying meal.

Crispy Taco-Stuffed Zucchini Boats with Salsa

Serves: 4
Prep time: 20 minutes / Cook time: 20 minutes

Ingredients:
- 4 medium zucchini
- 400g lean ground beef
- 1 small onion, diced
- 2 cloves garlic, minced
- 1 tbsp taco seasoning
- 120g shredded cheddar cheese
- 120ml salsa
- 60g sour cream
- Fresh cilantro leaves, for garnish

Preparation instructions:
1. Preheat the Air Fryer to 190°C for 5 minutes.
2. Cut each zucchini in half lengthwise and scoop out the centres to create a hollow boat shape.
3. In a skillet, cook the ground beef over medium heat until browned. Drain any excess fat.
4. Add the diced onion, minced garlic, and taco seasoning to the skillet. Cook for an additional 2-3 minutes until the onions are softened.
5. Fill each zucchini boat with the taco meat mixture.
6. Place the zucchini boats in the Air Fryer basket, ensuring they are not overlapping.
7. Air fry at 190°C for 15-20 minutes or until the zucchini is tender and the meat is cooked through.
8. Remove the zucchini boats from the Air Fryer and sprinkle shredded cheddar cheese on top of each boat.
9. Return the zucchini boats to the Air Fryer and air fry for an additional 2-3 minutes or until the cheese is melted and bubbly.
10. While the zucchini boats are cooking, prepare the salsa by combining the salsa and sour cream in a

bowl.

11. Once cooked, remove the zucchini boats from the Air Fryer and let them cool for a minute.
12. Drizzle the zucchini boats with salsa and sour cream mixture.
13. Garnish with fresh cilantro leaves.
14. Serve the crispy taco-stuffed zucchini boats as a flavorful and nutritious meal.

Italian Sausage and Pepper Hoagies with Spicy Mustard

Serves: 4
Prep time: 15 minutes / Cook time: 20 minutes

Ingredients:
- 4 Italian sausages
- 2 bell peppers, thinly sliced
- 1 small onion, thinly sliced
- 2 tbsp olive oil
- 1 tsp dried oregano
- 1/2 tsp dried basil
- 1/4 tsp red pepper flakes (optional)
- Salt and black pepper, to taste
- 4 hoagie rolls
- 4 tbsp spicy mustard

Preparation instructions:
1. Preheat the Air Fryer to 190°C for 5 minutes.
2. In a bowl, toss the sliced bell peppers and onions with olive oil, dried oregano, dried basil, red pepper flakes (if using), salt, and black pepper.
3. Place the seasoned bell peppers and onions in the Air Fryer basket.
4. Air fry at 190°C for 15-20 minutes or until the peppers and onions are tender and slightly caramelised.
5. While the peppers and onions are cooking, place the Italian sausages in the Air Fryer basket.
6. Air fry at 190°C for 15-20 minutes or until the sausages are cooked through and browned.
7. Once cooked, remove the sausages from the Air Fryer and let them rest for a minute. Then slice them diagonally into bite-sized pieces.
8. Slice the hoagie rolls lengthwise and spread spicy mustard on one side of each roll.
9. Fill each hoagie roll with the sliced sausages, roasted bell peppers, and onions.
10. Serve the Italian sausage and pepper hoagies as a

delicious and hearty meal.

BBQ Chicken Flatbread Pizzas with Caramelized Onions

Serves: 4
Prep time: 15 minutes / Cook time: 12 minutes

Ingredients:
- 4 flatbreads or naan breads
- 200g cooked chicken, shredded
- 120ml barbecue sauce
- 1 large onion, thinly sliced
- 2 tbsp olive oil
- 1 tsp balsamic vinegar
- 120g shredded mozzarella cheese
- Fresh cilantro leaves, for garnish

Preparation instructions:
1. Preheat the Air Fryer to 190°C for 5 minutes.
2. In a skillet, heat olive oil over medium heat. Add the sliced onions and cook until they are soft and caramelised, about 8-10 minutes.
3. Stir in the balsamic vinegar and cook for an additional 2 minutes.
4. In a bowl, combine the shredded chicken with barbecue sauce, mixing well to coat the chicken.
5. Place the flatbreads or naan breads in the Air Fryer basket.
6. Air fry at 190°C for 2-3 minutes to lightly toast the bread.
7. Remove the flatbreads from the Air Fryer and spread the caramelised onions evenly on each bread.
8. Top with the BBQ chicken mixture and sprinkle shredded mozzarella cheese on top.
9. Return the flatbreads to the Air Fryer and air fry at 190°C for 8-10 minutes or until the cheese is melted and bubbly.
10. Once cooked, remove the flatbread pizzas from the Air Fryer and let them cool for a minute.
11. Garnish with fresh cilantro leaves.
12. Serve the BBQ chicken flatbread pizzas as a tasty and satisfying meal.

Teriyaki Glazed Salmon Burgers with Asian Slaw

Serves: 4
Prep time: 15 minutes / Cook time: 12 minutes

Ingredients:

For the salmon burgers:
- 500g salmon fillets, skinless
- 30ml teriyaki sauce
- 2 tbsp breadcrumbs
- 1 green onion, finely chopped
- 1 garlic clove, minced
- 1 tbsp grated ginger
- 1/4 tsp salt
- 1/4 tsp black pepper
- 4 burger buns

For the Asian slaw:
- 200g shredded cabbage
- 1 carrot, julienned
- 1/2 red bell pepper, thinly sliced
- 2 green onions, thinly sliced
- 30ml rice vinegar
- 15ml soy sauce
- 1 tbsp sesame oil
- 1 tsp honey
- 1/4 tsp red pepper flakes (optional)

Preparation instructions:

1. Preheat the Air Fryer to 190°C for 5 minutes.
2. In a bowl, combine the salmon fillets, teriyaki sauce, breadcrumbs, green onion, minced garlic, grated ginger, salt, and black pepper. Mix well until the Ingredients are evenly incorporated.
3. Divide the salmon mixture into four equal portions and shape them into burger patties.
4. Place the salmon patties in the Air Fryer basket.
5. Air fry at 190°C for 10-12 minutes or until the salmon is cooked through and lightly browned.
6. While the salmon burgers are cooking, prepare the Asian slaw by combining shredded cabbage, julienned carrot, sliced red bell pepper, and sliced green onions in a bowl.
7. In a separate small bowl, whisk together rice vinegar, soy sauce, sesame oil, honey, and red pepper flakes (if using).
8. Pour the dressing over the slaw mixture and toss well to coat.
9. Toast the burger buns in the Air Fryer for 1-2 minutes until they are lightly crispy.
10. Assemble the salmon burgers by placing each patty on a toasted bun and topping it with a generous amount of Asian slaw.
11. Serve the teriyaki glazed salmon burgers with

Asian slaw as a delightful and healthy meal.

BBQ Bacon-Wrapped Stuffed Jalapenos with Cream Cheese

Serves: 4
Prep time: 20 minutes / Cook time: 12 minutes

Ingredients:
- 8 jalapeno peppers
- 100g cream cheese
- 8 slices bacon
- 60ml barbecue sauce
- Fresh cilantro leaves, for garnish

Preparation instructions:
1. Preheat the Air Fryer to 190°C for 5 minutes.
2. Cut each jalapeno pepper in half lengthwise and remove the seeds and membranes.
3. Fill each jalapeno half with cream cheese.
4. Wrap each jalapeno half with a slice of bacon, securing it with a toothpick if necessary.
5. Place the bacon-wrapped jalapenos in the Air Fryer basket, ensuring they are not overlapping.
6. Air fry at 190°C for 10-12 minutes or until the bacon is crispy and cooked through.
7. While the jalapenos are cooking, brush them with barbecue sauce halfway through the cooking time.
8. Once cooked, remove the bacon-wrapped jalapenos from the Air Fryer and let them cool for a minute.
9. Garnish with fresh cilantro leaves.
10. Serve the BBQ bacon-wrapped stuffed jalapenos as a spicy and savoury appetiser or snack.

Chicken Alfredo Stuffed Shells with Garlic Bread

Serves: 4
Prep time: 30 minutes / Cook time: 18 minutes

Ingredients:
- 200g jumbo pasta shells
- 300g cooked chicken, shredded
- 200g ricotta cheese
- 100g shredded mozzarella cheese
- 60g grated Parmesan cheese
- 1 egg, lightly beaten
- 240ml Alfredo sauce
- 1 garlic clove, minced

- 1/2 tsp dried basil
- 1/2 tsp dried oregano
- 1/4 tsp salt
- 1/4 tsp black pepper
- 4 slices garlic bread

Preparation instructions:

1. Preheat the Air Fryer to 190°C for 5 minutes.
2. Cook the jumbo pasta shells according to the package instructions until al dente. Drain and set aside.
3. In a bowl, combine the shredded chicken, ricotta cheese, shredded mozzarella cheese, grated Parmesan cheese, beaten egg, minced garlic, dried basil, dried oregano, salt, and black pepper. Mix well to form the filling mixture.
4. Stuff each cooked jumbo pasta shell with the chicken and cheese filling.
5. Pour half of the Alfredo sauce into the bottom of a baking dish. Arrange the stuffed shells in a single layer in the dish.
6. Drizzle the remaining Alfredo sauce over the stuffed shells.
7. Place the baking dish in the Air Fryer basket.
8. Air fry at 190°C for 15-18 minutes or until the shells are heated through and the sauce is bubbly.
9. While the stuffed shells are cooking, prepare the garlic bread according to the package instructions.
10. Once cooked, remove the baking dish from the Air Fryer and let it cool for a minute.
11. Serve the chicken Alfredo stuffed shells with a side of garlic bread for a comforting and delicious meal.

Black Bean Burgers with Chipotle Mayo

Serves: 2-4 people
Prep time: 15 minutes / Cook time: 12-15 minutes

Ingredients:

- 400g canned black beans, drained and rinsed
- 1 small onion, finely chopped
- 2 garlic cloves, minced
- 30g breadcrumbs
- 30g cornmeal
- 1 egg, beaten
- 5g ground cumin
- 5g chilli powder
- 2g paprika
- Salt and pepper to taste
- Olive oil (for cooking)
- Burger buns
- Lettuce, tomato, red onion (for topping)
- Chipotle mayo (for topping)

Preparation instructions:

1. In a large bowl, mash the black beans with a fork or potato masher until they are mostly mashed with some beans remaining intact.
2. Add the chopped onion, minced garlic, breadcrumbs, cornmeal, beaten egg, cumin, chilli powder, paprika, salt, and pepper to the bowl. Mix well to combine all the Ingredients.
3. Divide the mixture into equal portions and shape them into burger patties.
4. Preheat the air fryer to 200°C (400°F).
5. Lightly brush each burger patty with olive oil.
6. Place the patties in the air fryer basket, leaving space between them.
7. Air fry for 12-15 minutes, flipping the burgers halfway through, until they are golden brown and crispy.
8. While the burgers are cooking, prepare the chipotle mayo by combining mayonnaise with chipotle powder or adobo sauce. Adjust the spice level according to your preference.
9. Once the burgers are cooked, remove them from the air fryer and let them cool for a few minutes.
10. Assemble the Black Bean Burgers on burger buns, topped with lettuce, tomato, red onion, and a generous dollop of chipotle mayo.
11. Serve the burgers with your favourite side dishes, and enjoy!

Air Fryer Garlic Knots

Serves: 2-4 people
Prep time: 20-30 minutes | Cook time: 10 minutes

Ingredients:

- 450g pizza dough, homemade or store-bought
- 30g unsalted butter, melted
- 5g garlic powder
- 5g dried parsley
- Salt to taste

Preparation instructions:

1. Preheat the air fryer to 180°C (350°F).

2. On a lightly floured surface, roll out the pizza dough into a rectangle, about 1/2 inch thick.
3. Cut the dough into strips, approximately 1 inch wide.
4. Take each strip and tie it into a knot, tucking the ends underneath.
5. In a bowl, combine the melted butter, garlic powder, dried parsley, and salt. Mix well.
6. Dip each garlic knot into the butter mixture, ensuring they are evenly coated.
7. Place the coated garlic knots in the air fryer basket, leaving space between them.
8. Air fry for 8-10 minutes, or until the garlic knots are golden brown and cooked through.
9. Remove from the air fryer and let them cool for a few minutes.
10. Serve the air fryer garlic knots warm and enjoy!

Air Fryer Cornbread Muffins

Serves: 2-4 people
Prep time: 15-20 minutes | Cook time: 12-15 minutes

Ingredients:
- 120g cornmeal
- 120g all-purpose flour
- 50g granulated sugar
- 10g baking powder
- 2g salt
- 180 ml milk
- 60 ml vegetable oil
- 1 large egg

Preparation instructions:
1. Preheat the air fryer to 180°C (350°F).
2. In a bowl, whisk together the cornmeal, all-purpose flour, granulated sugar, baking powder, and salt.
3. In a separate bowl, whisk together the milk, vegetable oil, and egg.
4. Gradually add the wet Ingredients to the dry Ingredients, stirring until just combined. Do not overmix.
5. Grease a muffin tin or line it with paper liners.
6. Spoon the cornbread batter into the muffin cups, filling each about two-thirds full.
7. Place the muffin tin in the air fryer basket.
8. Air fry for 12-15 minutes, or until the cornbread muffins are golden brown and cooked through.

A toothpick inserted into the centre should come out clean.
9. Remove from the air fryer and let them cool for a few minutes.
10. Serve the air fryer cornbread muffins warm as a delightful side dish or a tasty snack.

Cinnamon Sugar Air Fryer Donut Holes

Serves: 2-6 people
Prep time: 20 minutes | Cook time: 6-8 minutes

Ingredients
- 200g all-purpose flour
- 5g baking powder
- 5g ground cinnamon
- 2g salt
- 80g granulated sugar
- 60 ml milk
- 30g unsalted butter, melted
- 1 large egg
- 5 ml vanilla extract
- 60g granulated sugar (for rolling)
- 5g ground cinnamon (for rolling)
- 60g unsalted butter, melted (for brushing)

Step-by-step guide
1. Preheat the air fryer to 180°C (350°F).
2. In a bowl, whisk together the all-purpose flour, baking powder, ground cinnamon, salt, and granulated sugar.
3. In a separate bowl, combine the milk, melted butter, egg, and vanilla extract. Mix well.
4. Gradually add the wet Ingredients to the dry Ingredients, stirring until just combined. Do not overmix.
5. Roll the dough into small, bite-sized balls, about 1 inch in diameter.
6. Place the donut holes in the air fryer basket, leaving space between them.
7. Air fry for 6-8 minutes, or until the donut holes are golden brown and cooked through.
8. While the donut holes are still warm, roll them in a mixture of granulated sugar and ground cinnamon until coated.
9. Brush the cinnamon sugar-coated donut holes with melted butter.
10. Serve the cinnamon-sugar air fryer donut holes warm and enjoy!

Chapter 7: Beans & Grains Recipes

Southwest Quinoa Stuffed Bell Peppers

Serves: 4
Prep time: 20 minutes / Cook time: 20 minutes

Ingredients:
- 4 bell peppers (assorted colours)
- 150g cooked quinoa
- 200g black beans, rinsed and drained
- 150g corn kernels
- 1 small red onion, diced
- 1 small jalapeno, seeded and finely chopped
- 2 cloves garlic, minced
- 1 tsp ground cumin
- 1 tsp chilli powder
- 1/2 tsp smoked paprika
- 1/4 tsp salt
- 1/4 tsp black pepper
- 60g shredded cheddar cheese
- Fresh cilantro, for garnish
- Sour cream, for serving (optional)

Preparation instructions:
1. Preheat the Air Fryer to 190°C for 5 minutes.
2. Cut the tops off the bell peppers and remove the seeds and membranes.
3. In a bowl, combine the cooked quinoa, black beans, corn kernels, diced red onion, jalapeno, minced garlic, ground cumin, chilli powder, smoked paprika, salt, and black pepper. Mix well to combine.
4. Spoon the quinoa mixture into each bell pepper until they are filled.
5. Place the stuffed bell peppers in the crisper basket of the Air Fryer.
6. Air fry at 190°C for 18-20 minutes or until the bell peppers are tender and slightly charred.
7. Sprinkle the shredded cheddar cheese over the top of each bell pepper and air fry for an additional 2 minutes or until the cheese is melted and bubbly.
8. Once cooked, remove the stuffed bell peppers from the Air Fryer and let them cool for a minute.
9. Garnish with fresh cilantro and serve with sour cream if desired.
10. Enjoy the Southwest quinoa stuffed bell peppers as a wholesome and flavorful meal.

Spicy Cajun Chickpea Fritters with Creole Aioli

Serves: 4
Prep time: 15 minutes / Cook time: 12 minutes

Ingredients:
- 200g canned chickpeas, drained and rinsed
- 1 small red bell pepper, diced
- 1/2 small red onion, diced
- 2 cloves garlic, minced
- 2 tbsp chopped fresh parsley
- 1 tsp Cajun seasoning
- 1/2 tsp paprika
- 1/4 tsp cayenne pepper
- 1/4 tsp salt
- 1/4 tsp black pepper
- 2 tbsp all-purpose flour
- 1 large egg, lightly beaten
- 60ml vegetable oil

For the Creole aioli:
- 4 tbsp mayonnaise
- 1 tbsp lemon juice
- 1 tsp Creole mustard
- 1/4 tsp garlic powder
- 1/4 tsp paprika
- 1/4 tsp hot sauce (optional)

Preparation instructions:
1. Preheat the Air Fryer to 190°C for 5 minutes.
2. In a bowl, mash the chickpeas with a fork or potato masher until they are mostly crushed but still have some texture.
3. Add the diced red bell pepper, diced red onion, minced garlic, chopped fresh parsley, Cajun seasoning, paprika, cayenne pepper, salt, black pepper, all-purpose flour, and lightly beaten egg to the bowl. Mix well to combine.
4. Shape the mixture into small fritters, about the size of a tablespoon.
5. Place the chickpea fritters in the crisper basket of the Air Fryer, ensuring they are not touching.
6. Drizzle the vegetable oil over the fritters.
7. Air fry at 190°C for 10-12 minutes or until the fritters are golden brown and crispy.
8. While the fritters are cooking, prepare the Creole

aioli by combining the mayonnaise, lemon juice, Creole mustard, garlic powder, paprika, and hot sauce (if using) in a small bowl. Mix well.

9. Once cooked, remove the chickpea fritters from the Air Fryer and let them cool for a minute.

10. Serve the spicy Cajun chickpea fritters with the Creole aioli as a tasty and satisfying appetiser or side dish.

Moroccan Spiced Lentil Burgers with Mint Yogurt Sauce

Serves: 4

Prep time: 20 minutes / Cook time: 15 minutes

Ingredients:

- 200g cooked lentils
- 1 small red onion, finely chopped
- 2 cloves garlic, minced
- 2 tbsp chopped fresh parsley
- 1 tsp ground cumin
- 1 tsp ground coriander
- 1/2 tsp ground cinnamon
- 1/2 tsp ground paprika
- 1/4 tsp ground turmeric
- 1/4 tsp salt
- 1/4 tsp black pepper
- 50g breadcrumbs
- 1 large egg, lightly beaten
- 60g plain flour
- 60ml vegetable oil
- For the mint yoghurt sauce:
- 150g Greek yoghurt
- 2 tbsp chopped fresh mint
- 1 tbsp lemon juice
- 1/4 tsp garlic powder
- Salt and black pepper, to taste

Preparation instructions:

1. Preheat the Air Fryer to 190°C for 5 minutes.

2. In a bowl, combine the cooked lentils, finely chopped red onion, minced garlic, chopped fresh parsley, ground cumin, ground coriander, ground cinnamon, ground paprika, ground turmeric, salt, black pepper, breadcrumbs, and lightly beaten egg. Mix well to form a mixture that holds together.

3. Shape the lentil mixture into patties, about 1/2-inch thick.

4. Place the lentil burgers in the crisper basket of the Air Fryer, ensuring they are not touching.

5. Dredge each lentil burger in the plain flour, shaking off any excess.

6. Drizzle the vegetable oil over the lentil burgers.

7. Air fry at 190°C for 12-15 minutes or until the burgers are crispy and heated through, flipping them halfway through cooking.

8. While the lentil burgers are cooking, prepare the mint yoghurt sauce by combining the Greek yoghurt, chopped fresh mint, lemon juice, garlic powder, salt, and black pepper in a small bowl. Mix well.

9. Once cooked, remove the lentil burgers from the Air Fryer and let them cool for a minute.

10. Serve the Moroccan spiced lentil burgers with the mint yoghurt sauce for a delicious and nutritious vegetarian meal.

Black Bean and Quinoa Veggie Burgers with Avocado Lime Aioli

Serves: 4

Prep time: 20 minutes / Cook time: 15 minutes

Ingredients:

- 200g cooked black beans
- 150g cooked quinoa
- 1 small red bell pepper, diced
- 1 small red onion, finely chopped
- 2 cloves garlic, minced
- 2 tbsp chopped fresh cilantro
- 1 tsp ground cumin
- 1 tsp chilli powder
- 1/2 tsp smoked paprika
- 1/4 tsp salt
- 1/4 tsp black pepper
- 50g breadcrumbs
- 1 large egg, lightly beaten
- 60g plain flour
- 60ml vegetable oil

For the avocado lime aioli:

- 1 ripe avocado
- 60g mayonnaise
- 1 tbsp lime juice
- 1/4 tsp garlic powder
- Salt and black pepper, to taste

Preparation instructions:

1. Preheat the Air Fryer to 190°C for 5 minutes.

2. In a bowl, mash the cooked black beans with

a fork or potato masher until they are mostly crushed but still have some texture.

3. Add the cooked quinoa, diced red bell pepper, finely chopped red onion, minced garlic, chopped fresh cilantro, ground cumin, chilli powder, smoked paprika, salt, black pepper, breadcrumbs, and lightly beaten egg to the bowl. Mix well to combine.
4. Shape the mixture into patties, about 1/2-inch thick.
5. Place the veggie burgers in the crisper basket of the Air Fryer, ensuring they are not touching.
6. Dredge each veggie burger in the plain flour, shaking off any excess.
7. Drizzle the vegetable oil over the veggie burgers.
8. Air fry at 190°C for 12-15 minutes or until the burgers are crispy and heated through, flipping them halfway through cooking.
9. While the veggie burgers are cooking, prepare the avocado lime aioli by mashing the ripe avocado in a small bowl. Add the mayonnaise, lime juice, garlic powder, salt, and black pepper. Mix well.
10. Once cooked, remove the veggie burgers from the Air Fryer and let them cool for a minute.
11. Serve the black bean and quinoa veggie burgers with the avocado lime aioli as a flavorful and satisfying vegetarian option.

Crispy Turmeric Rice Balls with Curry Dipping Sauce

Serves: 4
Prep time: 20 minutes / Cook time: 15 minutes

Ingredients:
- 200g cooked white rice
- 1 small red bell pepper, finely diced
- 1 small carrot, finely grated
- 2 spring onions, thinly sliced
- 2 tbsp chopped fresh cilantro
- 1 tsp ground turmeric
- 1/2 tsp ground cumin
- 1/2 tsp ground coriander
- 1/4 tsp salt
- 1/4 tsp black pepper
- 50g breadcrumbs
- 1 large egg, lightly beaten
- 60g plain flour
- 60ml vegetable oil

For the curry dipping sauce:
- 4 tbsp mayonnaise
- 2 tsp curry powder
- 1 tbsp lemon juice
- 1/4 tsp garlic powder
- Salt and black pepper, to taste

Preparation instructions:
1. Preheat the Air Fryer to 190°C for 5 minutes.
2. In a bowl, combine the cooked white rice, finely diced red bell pepper, finely grated carrot, thinly sliced spring onions, chopped fresh cilantro, ground turmeric, ground cumin, ground coriander, salt, black pepper, breadcrumbs, and lightly beaten egg. Mix well to form a sticky mixture.
3. Shape the mixture into small rice balls, about the size of a golf ball.
4. Place the rice balls in the crisper basket of the Air Fryer, ensuring they are not touching.
5. Dredge each rice ball in the plain flour, shaking off any excess.
6. Drizzle the vegetable oil over the rice balls.
7. Air fry at 190°C for 12-15 minutes or until the rice balls are crispy and golden brown, flipping them halfway through cooking.
8. While the rice balls are cooking, prepare the curry dipping sauce by combining the mayonnaise, curry powder, lemon juice, garlic powder, salt, and black pepper in a small bowl. Mix well.
9. Once cooked, remove the rice balls from the Air Fryer and let them cool for a minute.
10. Serve the crispy turmeric rice balls with the curry dipping sauce as a delightful snack or appetiser.

Cajun Red Beans and Rice Croquettes with Remoulade Sauce

Serves: 4
Prep time: 20 minutes / Cook time: 15 minutes

Ingredients:
- 200g cooked red beans
- 150g cooked rice
- 1 small green bell pepper, finely diced
- 1 small red onion, finely chopped
- 2 cloves garlic, minced
- 2 tbsp chopped fresh parsley
- 1 tsp Cajun seasoning
- 1/2 tsp paprika
- 1/4 tsp cayenne pepper
- 1/4 tsp salt
- 1/4 tsp black pepper

- 50g breadcrumbs
- 1 large egg, lightly beaten
- 60g plain flour
- 60ml vegetable oil

For the remoulade sauce:
- 4 tbsp mayonnaise
- 1 tbsp Dijon mustard
- 1 tbsp lemon juice
- 1 tsp hot sauce
- 2 tsp chopped fresh parsley
- 2 tsp chopped capers
- 1 clove garlic, minced
- Salt and black pepper, to taste

Preparation instructions:
1. Preheat the Air Fryer to 190°C for 5 minutes.
2. In a bowl, mash the cooked red beans with a fork or potato masher until they are mostly crushed but still have some texture.
3. Add the cooked rice, finely diced green bell pepper, finely chopped red onion, minced garlic, chopped fresh parsley, Cajun seasoning, paprika, cayenne pepper, salt, black pepper, breadcrumbs, and lightly beaten egg to the bowl. Mix well to combine.
4. Shape the mixture into croquettes, about 2 inches long.
5. Place the croquettes in the crisper basket of the Air Fryer, ensuring they are not touching.
6. Dredge each croquette in the plain flour, shaking off any excess.
7. Drizzle the vegetable oil over the croquettes.
8. Air fry at 190°C for 12-15 minutes or until the croquettes are crispy and heated through, flipping them halfway through cooking.
9. While the croquettes are cooking, prepare the remoulade sauce by combining the mayonnaise, Dijon mustard, lemon juice, hot sauce, chopped fresh parsley, chopped capers, minced garlic, salt, and black pepper in a small bowl. Mix well.
10. Once cooked, remove the croquettes from the Air Fryer and let them cool for a minute.
11. Serve the Cajun red beans and rice croquettes with the remoulade sauce for a flavorful and satisfying dish.

Greek-Style Baked Lima Beans with Feta and Olives

Serves: 4
Prep time: 15 minutes / Cook time: 25 minutes

Ingredients:
- 400g cooked lima beans
- 1 small red onion, finely chopped
- 2 cloves garlic, minced
- 2 tbsp chopped fresh parsley
- 1 tbsp chopped fresh dill
- 2 tbsp lemon juice
- 2 tbsp extra virgin olive oil
- 1/2 tsp dried oregano
- 1/4 tsp salt
- 1/4 tsp black pepper
- 50g crumbled feta cheese
- 50g pitted kalamata olives, halved

Preparation instructions:
1. Preheat the Air Fryer to 180°C for 5 minutes.
2. In a bowl, combine the cooked lima beans, finely chopped red onion, minced garlic, chopped fresh parsley, chopped fresh dill, lemon juice, extra virgin olive oil, dried oregano, salt, and black pepper. Mix well to combine.
3. Transfer the mixture to a baking dish that fits in the Air Fryer.
4. Place the baking dish in the Air Fryer.
5. Air fry at 180°C for 20-25 minutes or until the lima beans are heated through and slightly golden.
6. Sprinkle the crumbled feta cheese and halved kalamata olives over the top of the lima beans.
7. Air fry for an additional 2-3 minutes or until the cheese is slightly melted.
8. Once cooked, remove the Greek-style baked lima beans from the Air Fryer and let them cool for a minute.
9. Serve the Greek-style baked lima beans with feta and olives as a delicious and nutritious side dish or vegetarian main course.
10. Enjoy your Air Fryer culinary adventures!

Crispy Panko Crusted Wild Rice Cakes with Sriracha Mayo

Serves: 4
Prep time: 15 minutes / Cook time: 20 minutes

Ingredients:
- 200g cooked wild rice
- 50g panko breadcrumbs
- 30g grated Parmesan cheese
- 2 spring onions, finely chopped
- 2 tbsp chopped fresh parsley
- 1/2 tsp garlic powder

- 1/2 tsp onion powder
- 1/4 tsp salt
- 1/4 tsp black pepper
- 2 large eggs, beaten
- 60ml mayonnaise
- 1 tbsp sriracha sauce

Preparation instructions:
1. Preheat the Air Fryer to 200°C for 5 minutes.
2. In a bowl, combine the cooked wild rice, panko breadcrumbs, grated Parmesan cheese, finely chopped spring onions, chopped fresh parsley, garlic powder, onion powder, salt, and black pepper. Mix well to combine.
3. Shape the mixture into patties, about 2 inches in diameter.
4. Dip each patty into the beaten eggs, making sure to coat both sides.
5. Place the patties in the crisper basket of the Air Fryer, ensuring they are not touching.
6. Air fry at 200°C for 10 minutes, then flip the patties and air fry for an additional 10 minutes or until they are golden brown and crispy.
7. While the rice cakes are cooking, prepare the sriracha mayo by combining the mayonnaise and sriracha sauce in a small bowl. Mix well.
8. Once cooked, remove the wild rice cakes from the Air Fryer and let them cool for a minute.
9. Serve the crispy panko crusted wild rice cakes with the sriracha mayo for a delightful appetiser or side dish.

Spicy Chipotle Black Bean Tacos with Lime Slaw

Serves: 4
Prep time: 15 minutes / Cook time: 10 minutes

Ingredients:
For the chipotle black beans:
- 400g canned black beans, rinsed and drained
- 1 chipotle pepper in adobo sauce, minced
- 1 tbsp adobo sauce
- 1/2 tsp ground cumin
- 1/2 tsp chilli powder
- 1/4 tsp garlic powder
- 1/4 tsp onion powder
- Salt and black pepper, to taste
For the lime slaw:
- 200g shredded cabbage

- 2 spring onions, thinly sliced
- 2 tbsp chopped fresh cilantro
- Juice of 1 lime
- 1 tbsp extra virgin olive oil
- Salt and black pepper, to taste
For the tacos:
- 8 small corn tortillas
- 1 ripe avocado, sliced
- Fresh cilantro, for garnish
- Lime wedges, for serving

Preparation instructions:
1. Preheat the Air Fryer to 180°C for 5 minutes.
2. In a bowl, combine the rinsed and drained black beans, minced chipotle pepper, adobo sauce, ground cumin, chilli powder, garlic powder, onion powder, salt, and black pepper. Mix well to coat the beans with the spices.
3. Transfer the seasoned black beans to the crisper basket of the Air Fryer.
4. Air fry at 180°C for 8-10 minutes, stirring halfway through cooking, until the beans are heated through and slightly crispy.
5. While the beans are cooking, prepare the lime slaw by combining the shredded cabbage, thinly sliced spring onions, chopped fresh cilantro, lime juice, extra virgin olive oil, salt, and black pepper in a bowl. Toss well to combine.
6. Warm the corn tortillas in a dry skillet or microwave.
7. To assemble the tacos, spoon the spicy chipotle black beans onto each tortilla. Top with a generous amount of lime slaw, sliced avocado, and fresh cilantro.
8. Serve the spicy chipotle black bean tacos with lime wedges on the side for squeezing extra lime juice over the tacos, if desired.

Garlic Herb Farro Risotto with Roasted Vegetables

Serves: 4
Prep time: 10 minutes / Cook time: 25 minutes

Ingredients:
For the roasted vegetables:
- 200g cherry tomatoes
- 200g zucchini, diced
- 200g bell peppers, diced
- 2 tbsp olive oil
- 1/2 tsp garlic powder

- 1/2 tsp dried thyme
- 1/2 tsp dried rosemary
- Salt and black pepper, to taste

For the farro risotto:
- 200g farro
- 1 litre vegetable broth
- 2 tbsp butter
- 1 small onion, finely chopped
- 3 cloves garlic, minced
- 1/2 tsp dried thyme
- 1/2 tsp dried rosemary
- Salt and black pepper, to taste
- 2 tbsp grated Parmesan cheese
- 2 tbsp chopped fresh parsley, for garnish

Preparation instructions:
1. Preheat the Air Fryer to 200°C for 5 minutes.
2. In a bowl, toss together the cherry tomatoes, diced zucchini, diced bell peppers, olive oil, garlic powder, dried thyme, dried rosemary, salt, and black pepper.
3. Transfer the vegetables to the crisper basket of the Air Fryer.
4. Air fry at 200°C for 15-18 minutes, shaking the basket halfway through cooking, until the vegetables are roasted and tender.
5. While the vegetables are roasting, cook the farro according to the package instructions in vegetable broth until al dente. Drain any excess liquid and set aside.
6. In a large skillet, melt the butter over medium heat. Add the finely chopped onion and minced garlic. Sauté until the onion becomes translucent and the garlic is fragrant.
7. Stir in the cooked farro, dried thyme, dried rosemary, salt, and black pepper. Cook for 2-3 minutes, stirring occasionally, to allow the flavours to meld.
8. Remove the skillet from heat and stir in the grated Parmesan cheese. Mix until the cheese is melted and well combined.
9. Serve the garlic herb farro risotto topped with the roasted vegetables. Garnish with chopped fresh parsley.

Cajun Spiced Black Eyed Pea Fritters with Spicy Remoulade

Serves: 4
Prep time: 15 minutes / Cook time: 12 minutes

Ingredients:
For the black-eyed pea fritters:
- 400g canned black-eyed peas, drained and rinsed
- 1 small onion, finely chopped
- 1 small bell pepper, finely chopped
- 2 cloves garlic, minced
- 2 spring onions, thinly sliced
- 2 tbsp chopped fresh parsley
- 1 tsp Cajun seasoning
- 1/2 tsp smoked paprika
- 1/2 tsp garlic powder
- 1/2 tsp onion powder
- Salt and black pepper, to taste
- 60g breadcrumbs
- 2 eggs, beaten
- Vegetable oil, for frying

For the spicy remoulade:
- 100g mayonnaise
- 2 tbsp Dijon mustard
- 1 tbsp hot sauce
- 1 tbsp chopped fresh parsley
- 1 tbsp chopped fresh chives
- 1 tsp Worcestershire sauce
- Juice of 1/2 lemon
- Salt and black pepper, to taste

Preparation instructions:
1. In a large bowl, mash the drained and rinsed black-eyed peas with a fork or potato masher.
2. Add the finely chopped onion, finely chopped bell pepper, minced garlic, thinly sliced spring onions, chopped fresh parsley, Cajun seasoning, smoked paprika, garlic powder, onion powder, salt, and black pepper to the bowl. Mix well to combine.
3. Gradually add the breadcrumbs and beaten eggs to the mixture, stirring until well incorporated. The mixture should hold together but still be slightly sticky.
4. Shape the mixture into small patties, about 2 inches in diameter.
5. Preheat the Air Fryer to 180°C for 5 minutes.
6. Lightly brush or spray the patties with vegetable oil.
7. Place the patties in the crisper basket of the Air Fryer, ensuring they are not touching.
8. Air fry at 180°C for 10-12 minutes, flipping halfway through cooking, until the fritters are golden brown and crispy.
9. While the fritters are cooking, prepare the spicy

remoulade by combining the mayonnaise, Dijon mustard, hot sauce, chopped fresh parsley, chopped fresh chives, Worcestershire sauce, lemon juice, salt, and black pepper in a small bowl. Mix well.

10. Serve the Cajun spiced black-eyed pea fritters with the spicy remoulade sauce for dipping. They make a delicious appetiser or side dish.

Cheesy Broccoli and Rice Patties with Roasted Red Pepper Sauce

Serves: 4
Prep time: 20 minutes / Cook time: 15 minutes

Ingredients:

For the broccoli and rice patties:

- 200g cooked rice
- 200g cooked broccoli florets, finely chopped
- 100g grated cheddar cheese
- 2 spring onions, thinly sliced
- 2 cloves garlic, minced
- 2 tbsp chopped fresh parsley
- 2 tbsp breadcrumbs
- 2 eggs, beaten
- 1/2 tsp garlic powder
- 1/2 tsp onion powder
- Salt and black pepper, to taste
- Vegetable oil, for frying

For the roasted red pepper sauce:

- 2 roasted red peppers, peeled and seeded
- 2 tbsp mayonnaise
- 1 tbsp lemon juice
- 1 clove garlic, minced
- Salt and black pepper, to taste

Preparation instructions:

1. In a large bowl, combine the cooked rice, finely chopped cooked broccoli florets, grated cheddar cheese, thinly sliced spring onions, minced garlic, chopped fresh parsley, breadcrumbs, beaten eggs, garlic powder, onion powder, salt, and black pepper. Mix well to combine.

2. Shape the mixture into patties, about 2 inches in diameter.

3. Preheat the Air Fryer to 200°C for 5 minutes.

4. Lightly brush or spray the patties with vegetable oil.

5. Place the patties in the crisper basket of the Air Fryer, ensuring they are not touching.

6. Air fry at 200°C for 12-15 minutes, flipping halfway through cooking, until the patties are golden brown and crispy.

7. While the patties are cooking, prepare the roasted red pepper sauce by combining the roasted red peppers, mayonnaise, lemon juice, minced garlic, salt, and black pepper in a blender or food processor. Blend until smooth.

8. Serve the cheesy broccoli and rice patties with the roasted red pepper sauce for dipping. They make a delicious vegetarian meal or appetiser.

Spiced Chickpea and Bulgur Wheat Pilaf with Yogurt Sauce

Serves: 4
Prep time: 15 minutes / Cook time: 20 minutes

Ingredients:

For the pilaf:

- 200g cooked bulgur wheat
- 200g canned chickpeas, rinsed and drained
- 1 small onion, finely chopped
- 2 cloves garlic, minced
- 1/2 tsp ground cumin
- 1/2 tsp ground coriander
- 1/2 tsp paprika
- 1/4 tsp turmeric
- 1/4 tsp cinnamon
- Salt and black pepper, to taste
- 2 tbsp chopped fresh parsley
- 2 tbsp lemon juice

For the yoghurt sauce:

- 150g Greek yoghurt
- 1 tbsp lemon juice
- 1 clove garlic, minced
- 1 tbsp chopped fresh mint
- Salt and black pepper, to taste

Preparation instructions:

1. In a skillet, heat a small amount of oil over medium heat. Add the finely chopped onion and minced garlic. Sauté until the onion becomes translucent and the garlic is fragrant.

2. Add the ground cumin, ground coriander, paprika, turmeric, cinnamon, salt, and black pepper to the skillet. Stir well to coat the onions and garlic with the spices.

3. Add the cooked bulgur wheat and rinsed chickpeas to the skillet. Stir to combine all the Ingredients.

4. Cook for 5 minutes, stirring occasionally, until the mixture is heated through and the flavours are well blended.
5. Remove the skillet from heat and stir in the chopped fresh parsley and lemon juice.
6. Preheat the Air Fryer to 180°C for 5 minutes.
7. Transfer the pilaf mixture to the crisper basket of the Air Fryer.
8. Air fry at 180°C for 10-12 minutes, stirring once or twice, until the pilaf is heated through and slightly crispy.
9. While the pilaf is cooking, prepare the yoghurt sauce by combining the Greek yoghurt, lemon juice, minced garlic, chopped fresh mint, salt, and black pepper in a small bowl. Mix well.
10. Serve the spiced chickpea and bulgur wheat pilaf with the yoghurt sauce on the side. It's a flavorful and satisfying vegetarian dish.

Crispy Quinoa and Vegetable Spring Rolls with Peanut Dipping Sauce

Serves: 4
Prep time: 30 minutes / Cook time: 15 minutes

Ingredients:
For the spring rolls:
- 100g cooked quinoa
- 200g mixed vegetables (carrots, cabbage, bell peppers, etc.), julienned
- 2 spring onions, thinly sliced
- 2 cloves garlic, minced
- 1 tbsp soy sauce
- 1/2 tsp sesame oil
- 1/4 tsp ground ginger
- 1/4 tsp garlic powder
- 1/4 tsp onion powder
- Salt and black pepper, to taste
- 8 spring roll wrappers
- Water, for sealing the wrappers
- Vegetable oil, for frying

For the peanut dipping sauce:
- 60g creamy peanut butter
- 2 tbsp soy sauce
- 1 tbsp rice vinegar
- 1 tbsp honey or maple syrup
- 1 clove garlic, minced
- 1/2 tsp grated ginger

- Hot water, as needed to thin the sauce

Preparation instructions:
1. In a large bowl, combine the cooked quinoa, julienned mixed vegetables, thinly sliced spring onions, minced garlic, soy sauce, sesame oil, ground ginger, garlic powder, onion powder, salt, and black pepper. Mix well to combine.
2. Place a spring roll wrapper on a clean surface. Spoon about 2 tablespoons of the quinoa and vegetable mixture onto the centre of the wrapper.
3. Fold the sides of the wrapper towards the centre, then roll up tightly, sealing the edges with water.
4. Repeat the process with the remaining spring roll wrappers and filling.
5. Preheat the Air Fryer to 200°C for 5 minutes.
6. Lightly brush or spray the spring rolls with vegetable oil.
7. Place the spring rolls in the crisper basket of the Air Fryer, ensuring they are not touching.
8. Air fry at 200°C for 12-15 minutes, flipping halfway through cooking, until the spring rolls are golden brown and crispy.
9. While the spring rolls are cooking, prepare the peanut dipping sauce by combining the creamy peanut butter, soy sauce, rice vinegar, honey or maple syrup, minced garlic, and grated ginger in a small bowl. Mix well. Add hot water gradually, stirring, until the sauce reaches a desired consistency.
10. Serve the crispy quinoa and vegetable spring rolls with the peanut dipping sauce. They make a delicious appetiser or light meal.

Crispy Pinto Bean and Brown Rice Cakes with Cilantro Lime Sauce

Serves: 4
Prep time: 20 minutes / Cook time: 15 minutes

Ingredients:
For the pinto bean and brown rice cakes:
- 200g cooked brown rice
- 200g cooked pinto beans, drained and rinsed
- 1 small onion, finely chopped
- 2 cloves garlic, minced
- 2 tbsp chopped fresh cilantro
- 2 tbsp breadcrumbs
- 1 tsp ground cumin
- 1/2 tsp chilli powder
- 1/4 tsp smoked paprika

- Salt and black pepper, to taste
- Vegetable oil, for frying

For the cilantro lime sauce:
- 100g Greek yoghurt
- 1 tbsp lime juice
- 2 tbsp chopped fresh cilantro
- 1 clove garlic, minced
- Salt and black pepper, to taste

Preparation instructions:
1. In a large bowl, mash the cooked pinto beans with a fork or potato masher.
2. Add the cooked brown rice, finely chopped onion, minced garlic, chopped fresh cilantro, breadcrumbs, ground cumin, chilli powder, smoked paprika, salt, and black pepper to the bowl. Mix well to combine.
3. Shape the mixture into patties, about 2 inches in diameter.
4. Preheat the Air Fryer to 200°C for 5 minutes.
5. Lightly brush or spray the patties with vegetable oil.
6. Place the patties in the crisper basket of the Air Fryer, ensuring they are not touching.
7. Air fry at 200°C for 12-15 minutes, flipping halfway through cooking, until the cakes are golden brown and crispy.
8. While the cakes are cooking, prepare the cilantro lime sauce by combining the Greek yoghurt, lime juice, chopped fresh cilantro, minced garlic, salt, and black pepper in a small bowl. Mix well.
9. Serve the crispy pinto bean and brown rice cakes with the cilantro lime sauce. They make a tasty vegetarian meal or appetiser.

Spicy Black Bean Tacos with Avocado Crema

Serves: 2-4 people
Prep time: 15-20 minutes | Cook time: 10-12 minutes

Ingredients:
- 1 can (400g) black beans, drained and rinsed
- 5g chilli powder
- 5g cumin
- 2g paprika
- 2g garlic powder
- 2g onion powder
- 2g salt

- 30 ml olive oil
- 8 small tortillas
- Shredded lettuce (for topping)
- Chopped tomatoes (for topping)
- Chopped cilantro (for topping)
- Lime wedges (for serving)
- Avocado Crema
- 1 ripe avocado
- 60 ml sour cream (or Greek yoghurt for a healthier option)
- 15 ml lime juice
- Salt to taste

Preparation instructions:
1. Preheat the air fryer to 200°C (400°F).
2. In a bowl, combine the black beans, chilli powder, cumin, paprika, garlic powder, onion powder, salt, and olive oil. Mix well to coat the beans with the spice mixture.
3. Place the seasoned black beans in the air fryer basket.
4. Air fry for 10-12 minutes, shaking the basket halfway through, until the black beans are heated through and slightly crispy.
5. Meanwhile, prepare the avocado crema. In a blender or food processor, combine the ripe avocado, sour cream, lime juice, and salt. Blend until smooth and creamy.
6. Warm the tortillas according to package instructions.
7. To assemble the tacos, spread a spoonful of the avocado crema on each tortilla.
8. Top with the crispy black beans, shredded lettuce, chopped tomatoes, and chopped cilantro.
9. Squeeze fresh lime juice over the tacos for an extra burst of flavour.
10. Serve the Spicy Black Bean Tacos with Avocado Crema as a delicious and satisfying vegetarian meal.

Air Fryer Falafel with Tahini Sauce

Serves: 2-4 people
Prep time: 12-15 minutes | Cook time: 15 minutes

Ingredients
- 250g canned chickpeas, drained and rinsed
- 1 small onion, roughly chopped
- 3 garlic cloves, minced
- 15g fresh parsley, chopped
- 15g fresh cilantro, chopped
- 5g ground cumin
- 5g ground coriander

- 2g baking powder
- 15g all-purpose flour
- Salt and pepper to taste
- Olive oil (for brushing)
- Pita bread, lettuce, tomatoes, and cucumber (for serving)
- Tahini sauce (for serving)

Preparation instructions:

1. In a food processor, combine the chickpeas, onion, garlic, parsley, cilantro, cumin, coriander, baking powder, flour, salt, and pepper. Pulse until the mixture is well combined and forms a coarse texture.
2. Shape the mixture into small falafel balls, about 1 inch in diameter.
3. Preheat the air fryer to 200°C (400°F).
4. Lightly brush the falafel balls with olive oil.
5. Place the falafel balls in the air fryer basket, leaving space between them.
6. Air fry for 12-15 minutes, flipping the falafel halfway through, until they are golden brown and crispy.
7. While the falafel is cooking, prepare the tahini sauce by combining tahini paste with lemon juice, garlic, salt, and water. Whisk until smooth and creamy.
8. Once the falafel is cooked, remove them from the air fryer and let them cool for a few minutes.
9. Serve the air-fried falafel with warm pita bread, lettuce, tomatoes, and cucumber, and drizzle with tahini sauce.

Crispy Air Fryer Lentil Fritters

Serves: 2-4 people
Prep time: 10 minutes | Cook time: 10-12 minutes

Ingredients

- 250g cooked lentils (green or red), drained
- 1 small onion, finely chopped
- 2 garlic cloves, minced
- 15g fresh cilantro, chopped
- 5g ground cumin
- 5g ground coriander
- 2g paprika
- 2g chilli powder
- Salt and pepper to taste
- 30g breadcrumbs
- Olive oil (for brushing)

Preparation instructions:

1. In a mixing bowl, combine the cooked lentils,

chopped onion, minced garlic, chopped cilantro, cumin, coriander, paprika, chilli powder, salt, pepper, and breadcrumbs. Mix well until all the Ingredients are evenly incorporated.
2. Shape the mixture into small fritter patties.
3. Preheat the air fryer to 200°C (400°F).
4. Lightly brush each fritter with olive oil.
5. Place the fritters in the air fryer basket, leaving space between them.
6. Air fry for 10-12 minutes, flipping the fritters halfway through, until they are golden brown and crispy.
7. Once the fritters are cooked, remove them from the air fryer and let them cool for a few minutes.
8. Serve the crispy air-fried lentil fritters as a delicious appetiser or snack. They pair well with yoghurt sauce or a tangy chutney for dipping.

Air Fryer Refried Beans

Serves: 2-4 people
Prep time: 5-7 minutes | Cook time: 8-10 minutes

Ingredients

- 400g canned pinto beans, drained and rinsed
- 1 small onion, chopped
- 2 garlic cloves, minced
- 30 ml olive oil
- 5g ground cumin
- 5g chilli powder
- 2g paprika
- Salt and pepper to taste
- Fresh cilantro (for garnish)

Preparation instructions:

1. In a skillet, heat the olive oil over medium heat.
2. Add the chopped onion and minced garlic to the skillet. Sauté until the onion becomes translucent and fragrant.
3. Add the drained pinto beans to the skillet, along with cumin, chilli powder, paprika, salt, and pepper. Mix well to combine all the Ingredients.
4. Cook the beans for a few minutes, stirring occasionally, until they are heated through and well coated with the spices.
5. Transfer the bean mixture to the air fryer basket.
6. Preheat the air fryer to 180°C (350°F).
7. Air fry the beans for 8-10 minutes, stirring halfway through, until they are slightly crispy and golden.
8. Remove the refried beans from the air fryer and

let them cool for a few minutes.

9. Garnish with fresh cilantro before serving.

10. Serve the air-fried refried beans as a side dish alongside tacos, burritos, or as a flavorful dip for tortilla chips.

Cajun Seasoned Air Fryer Pinto Beans

Serves: 2-6 people
Prep time: 5 minutes | Cook time: 10-12 minutes

Ingredients

- 400g canned pinto beans, drained and rinsed
- 15 ml olive oil
- 5g Cajun seasoning
- 2g garlic powder
- 2g onion powder
- 2g paprika
- 2g cayenne pepper (adjust according to spice preference)
- Salt to taste

Preparation instructions:

1. In a mixing bowl, combine the drained pinto beans, olive oil, Cajun seasoning, garlic powder, onion powder, paprika, cayenne pepper, and salt. Toss well to coat the beans evenly with the spices.

2. Preheat the air fryer to 200°C (400°F).

3. Spread the seasoned beans in a single layer in the air fryer basket.

4. Air fry for 10-12 minutes, shaking the basket or stirring the beans halfway through the cooking time, until they are crispy and golden.

5. Once the beans are cooked to your desired crispiness, remove them from the air fryer and let them cool for a few minutes.

6. Serve the Cajun Seasoned Air Fryer Pinto Beans as a crunchy snack or use them as a topping for salads, bowls, or tacos.

Garlic Parmesan Edamame

Serves: 2-4 people
Prep time: 5 minutes | Cook time: 10-12 minutes

Ingredients

- 300g frozen edamame, thawed
- 15 ml olive oil
- 2 garlic cloves, minced
- 30g grated Parmesan cheese
- Salt and pepper to taste
- Fresh parsley (for garnish)

Preparation instructions:

1. In a mixing bowl, combine the thawed edamame, olive oil, minced garlic, grated Parmesan cheese, salt, and pepper. Toss well to coat the edamame evenly with the seasoning.

2. Preheat the air fryer to 200°C (400°F).

3. Spread the seasoned edamame in a single layer in the air fryer basket.

4. Air fry for 10-12 minutes, shaking the basket or stirring the edamame halfway through the cooking time, until they are crispy and slightly golden.

5. Once the edamame is cooked, remove them from the air fryer and let them cool for a few minutes.

6. Garnish with fresh parsley before serving.

7. Serve the Garlic Parmesan Edamame as a flavorful appetiser or snack. They are perfect for sharing and can be enjoyed warm or at room temperature.

BBQ Baked Beans with a Crunchy Topping

Serves: 2-4 people
Prep time: 10 minutes | Cook time: 10-12 minutes

Ingredients

- 400g canned baked beans
- 60 ml BBQ sauce
- 15g brown sugar
- 15 ml Worcestershire sauce
- 5g Dijon mustard
- 60g breadcrumbs
- 30g cooked bacon, crumbled
- Salt and pepper to taste

Preparation instructions:

1. In a mixing bowl, combine the baked beans, BBQ sauce, brown sugar, Worcestershire sauce, and Dijon mustard. Mix well to ensure the beans are evenly coated in the sauce.

2. Transfer the bean mixture to an oven-safe dish.

3. In a separate bowl, mix the breadcrumbs, crumbled bacon, salt, and pepper.

4. Sprinkle the breadcrumb and bacon mixture evenly over the top of the beans.

5. Preheat the air fryer to 180°C (350°F).

6. Place the dish with the beans in the air fryer basket.

7. Air fry for 10-12 minutes, until the topping is

golden brown and crispy.

8. Once cooked, remove the dish from the air fryer and let it cool for a few minutes before serving.

9. Serve the BBQ Baked Beans with a Crunchy Topping as a flavorful side dish or even as a main course. They pair well with grilled meats, sandwiches, or enjoyed on their own.

Air Fryer Mexican Street Corn with Black Bean Salsa

Serves: 2-4 people
Prep time: 15 minutes | Cook time: 12-15 minutes

Ingredients

For the Mexican Street Corn

- 4 ears of corn, husked
- 60 ml mayonnaise
- 60g sour cream
- 15 ml lime juice
- 5g chilli powder
- 5g smoked paprika
- 30g grated Parmesan cheese
- Fresh cilantro, chopped (for garnish)

For the Black Bean Salsa

- 200g canned black beans, drained and rinsed
- 1 small red bell pepper, diced
- 1 small red onion, diced
- 1 jalapeno pepper, seeded and diced
- 15 ml lime juice
- 15 ml olive oil
- Salt and pepper to taste

Preparation instructions:

1. Preheat the air fryer to 200°C (400°F).

2. In a small bowl, mix together the mayonnaise, sour cream, lime juice, chilli powder, smoked paprika, and grated Parmesan cheese to make the sauce for the Mexican street corn. Set aside.

3. Place the husked corn in the air fryer basket.

4. Air fry the corn for 12–15 minutes, turning the ears occasionally, until they are lightly charred and cooked through.

5. While the corn is cooking, prepare the black bean salsa. In a separate bowl, combine the black beans, diced red bell pepper, diced red onion, diced jalapeno pepper, lime juice, olive oil, salt, and pepper. Mix well.

6. Once the corn is cooked, remove it from the air

fryer and let it cool for a few minutes.

7. Slather each ear of corn with the prepared sauce, ensuring it is fully coated.

8. Sprinkle the corn with the black bean salsa and garnish with fresh cilantro.

9. Serve the Air Fryer Mexican Street Corn with Black Bean Salsa as a delicious and vibrant side dish or appetiser. Enjoy it while it's still warm.

Crispy Air Fryer Falafel Sliders

Serves: 2-4 people
Prep time: 15-20 minutes | Cook time: 12-15 minutes

Ingredients

For the falafel

- 400g canned chickpeas, drained and rinsed
- 1 small onion, chopped
- 3 garlic cloves, minced
- 30g fresh parsley, chopped
- 15g fresh cilantro, chopped
- 15 ml lemon juice
- 30g breadcrumbs
- 5g ground cumin
- 5g ground coriander
- Salt and pepper to taste

For the sliders

- Mini slider buns
- Lettuce leaves
- Sliced tomatoes
- Sliced cucumbers
- Tzatziki sauce or tahini sauce (optional)

Preparation instructions:

1. In a food processor, combine the drained chickpeas, chopped onion, minced garlic, fresh parsley, fresh cilantro, lemon juice, breadcrumbs, ground cumin, ground coriander, salt, and pepper. Pulse until the mixture comes together but is still slightly coarse.

2. Shape the falafel mixture into small patties, approximately the size of a slider bun.

3. Preheat the air fryer to 180°C (350°F).

4. Place the falafel patties in the air fryer basket, ensuring they are not overcrowded.

5. Air fry for 12-15 minutes, flipping the patties halfway through, until they are golden brown and crispy.

6. Once cooked, remove the falafel patties from the

air fryer and let them cool for a few minutes.

7. Assemble the falafel sliders by placing a falafel patty on a mini slider bun.

8. Top with lettuce leaves, sliced tomatoes, sliced cucumbers, and a drizzle of tzatziki sauce or tahini sauce, if desired.

9. Serve the crispy, air-fried falafel sliders as a delightful and satisfying meal. They are perfect for parties, picnics, or a quick and flavorful lunch.

Air Fryer Three Bean Salad

Serves: 2-4 people
Prep time: 15-20 minutes | Cook time: 10-12 minutes

Ingredients

- 200g canned kidney beans, drained and rinsed
- 200g canned chickpeas, drained and rinsed
- 200g canned black beans, drained and rinsed
- 1 small red onion, finely chopped
- 1 small red bell pepper, diced
- 1 small green bell pepper, diced
- 60 ml apple cider vinegar
- 30 ml olive oil
- 15 ml Dijon mustard
- 5g sugar
- Salt and pepper to taste
- Fresh parsley, chopped (for garnish)

Preparation instructions:

1. Preheat the air fryer to 200°C (400°F).

2. In a mixing bowl, combine the drained kidney beans, chickpeas, and black beans.

3. Place the mixed beans in the air fryer basket and spread them out in a single layer.

4. Air fry for 10-12 minutes, shaking the basket halfway through, until the beans are crispy and lightly golden.

5. While the beans are roasting, prepare the dressing by whisking together apple cider vinegar, olive oil, Dijon mustard, sugar, salt, and pepper in a small bowl.

6. In a large bowl, combine the roasted beans, chopped red onion, diced red bell pepper, diced green bell pepper, and the prepared dressing. Mix well to coat all the Ingredients.

7. Let the salad marinate in the refrigerator for at least 30 minutes to allow the flavours to meld together.

8. Before serving, garnish with fresh chopped parsley.

9. Serve the Air Fryer Three Bean Salad chilled as a nutritious and flavorful side dish or as a light and refreshing meal.

Smoky Air Fryer Red Lentil Dip

Serves: 2-4 people
Prep time: 10 minutes | Cook time: 10-12 minutes

Ingredients

- 200g dried red lentils, rinsed
- 500 ml vegetable broth
- 2 garlic cloves, minced
- 30 ml olive oil
- 15 ml lemon juice
- 5g smoked paprika
- 5g ground cumin
- Salt and pepper to taste
- Fresh cilantro (for garnish)

Preparation instructions:

1. In a saucepan, bring the vegetable broth to a boil and add the red lentils. Cook the lentils according to the package instructions until they are tender.

2. Drain any excess liquid from the cooked lentils and let them cool slightly.

3. Preheat the air fryer to 200°C (400°F).

4. In a mixing bowl, combine the cooked lentils, minced garlic, olive oil, lemon juice, smoked paprika, ground cumin, salt, and pepper. Mix well to incorporate all the flavours.

5. Place the lentil mixture in the air fryer basket and spread it out evenly.

6. Air fry for 10-12 minutes, stirring the mixture halfway through, until it becomes crispy and golden.

7. Once cooked, remove the lentil dip from the air fryer and let it cool for a few minutes.

8. Garnish with fresh cilantro before serving.

9. Serve the Smoky Air Fryer Red Lentil Dip as a flavorful dip with your favourite crackers, chips, or vegetable sticks.

Spicy Cajun Roasted Chickpeas

Serves: 2-4 people
Prep time: 5-10 minutes | Cook time: 15-20 minutes

Ingredients

- 400g canned chickpeas, drained and rinsed
- 15 ml olive oil
- 5g Cajun seasoning
- 5g paprika
- 2g garlic powder
- 2g onion powder
- 2g cayenne pepper (adjust to your desired spice level)
- Salt to taste

Preparation instructions:

1. Preheat the air fryer to 200°C (400°F).
2. Pat dry the drained and rinsed chickpeas using a paper towel to remove any excess moisture.
3. In a bowl, toss the chickpeas with olive oil, Cajun seasoning, paprika, garlic powder, onion powder, cayenne pepper, and salt. Ensure that the chickpeas are well coated with the seasoning.
4. Place the seasoned chickpeas in the air fryer basket, spreading them out in a single layer.
5. Air fry for 15-20 minutes, shaking the basket occasionally to ensure even cooking, until the chickpeas become crispy and golden.
6. Once cooked, remove the chickpeas from the air fryer and let them cool for a few minutes.
7. Serve the Spicy Cajun Roasted Chickpeas as a flavorful and addictive snack. Enjoy them on their own or add them to salads, trail mixes, or as a topping for soups and stews.

Buffalo Ranch Roasted Chickpeas

Serves: 2-4 people
Prep time: 5 minutes | Cook time: 12-15 minutes

Ingredients

- 400g canned chickpeas, drained and rinsed
- 30 ml buffalo sauce
- 15 ml olive oil
- 5g ranch seasoning
- Salt to taste

Preparation instructions:

1. Preheat the air fryer to 200°C (400°F).
2. In a mixing bowl, combine the chickpeas, buffalo sauce, olive oil, ranch seasoning, and salt. Toss well to ensure the chickpeas are evenly coated in the sauce and seasoning.
3. Place the seasoned chickpeas in the air fryer

basket, spreading them out in a single layer.
4. Air fry for 12-15 minutes, shaking the basket or stirring the chickpeas halfway through the cooking time, until they are crispy and slightly browned.
5. Once cooked, remove the chickpeas from the air fryer and let them cool for a few minutes.
6. Serve the Buffalo Ranch Roasted Chickpeas as a flavorful snack or party appetiser. They are best enjoyed when they are still warm and crispy.

Stuffed Air Fryer Bell Peppers with Rice

Serves: 2-4 people
Prep time: 20 minutes | Cook time: 15-20 minutes

Ingredients

- 4 bell peppers (any colour), tops removed and seeds removed
- 120g cooked rice
- 60g diced tomatoes
- 60g diced onions
- 60g diced zucchini
- 60g diced mushrooms
- 60g shredded cheddar cheese
- 5g dried basil
- 5g dried oregano
- Salt and pepper to taste
- Olive oil for brushing

Preparation instructions:

1. Preheat the air fryer to 180°C (350°F).
2. In a bowl, combine the cooked rice, diced tomatoes, diced onions, diced zucchini, diced mushrooms, shredded cheddar cheese, dried basil, dried oregano, salt, and pepper. Mix well.
3. Stuff each bell pepper with the rice and vegetable mixture, pressing it down lightly.
4. Brush the bell peppers with olive oil to coat the skins.
5. Place the stuffed bell peppers in the air fryer basket.
6. Air fry for 15-20 minutes, or until the bell peppers are tender and the stuffing is heated through.
7. Remove from the air fryer and let them cool for a few minutes.
8. Serve the stuffed air fryer bell peppers hot as a delicious and wholesome meal.

Chapter 8: Appetisers and Sides

Zucchini Ribbon Fritters with Spicy Marinara Sauce

Serves: 4
Prep time: 20 minutes / Cook time: 10 minutes

Ingredients:

- 2 large zucchinis
- 1 tsp salt
- 60g all-purpose flour
- 2 large eggs
- 30g grated Parmesan cheese
- 2 cloves garlic, minced
- 2 tbsp chopped fresh parsley
- 1/4 tsp black pepper
- Vegetable oil, for frying
- For the spicy marinara sauce:
- 200g tomato passata
- 1 clove garlic, minced
- 1/2 tsp dried oregano
- 1/4 tsp red pepper flakes (adjust to taste)
- Salt and black pepper, to taste

Preparation instructions:

1. Using a vegetable peeler, slice the zucchinis lengthwise into thin ribbons. Place the ribbons in a colander, sprinkle with salt, and let them sit for 10 minutes to release excess moisture. After 10 minutes, pat the zucchini ribbons dry with paper towels.
2. In a large bowl, whisk together the all-purpose flour, eggs, grated Parmesan cheese, minced garlic, chopped fresh parsley, and black pepper until well combined.
3. Add the zucchini ribbons to the bowl and gently toss until they are evenly coated with the batter.
4. Preheat the Air Fryer to 200°C for 5 minutes.
5. Lightly brush or spray the Air Fryer basket with vegetable oil.
6. Take a small handful of the zucchini ribbons, squeeze out any excess batter, and place them in a single layer in the Air Fryer basket. Repeat with the remaining zucchini ribbons.
7. Air fry at 200°C for 8-10 minutes, flipping halfway through cooking, until the fritters are golden brown and crispy.
8. While the fritters are cooking, prepare the spicy marinara sauce. In a small saucepan, combine the tomato passata, minced garlic, dried oregano, red pepper flakes, salt, and black pepper. Heat over medium heat until warmed through.
9. Serve the zucchini ribbon fritters with the spicy marinara sauce. They make a delicious appetiser or side dish.

Crispy Bacon-Wrapped Asparagus Bundles with Balsamic Glaze

Serves: 4
Prep time: 15 minutes / Cook time: 10 minutes

Ingredients:

- 16 asparagus spears
- 8 slices bacon
- 1 tbsp olive oil
- Salt and black pepper, to taste
- 2 tbsp balsamic glaze, for drizzling

Preparation instructions:

1. Trim the tough ends of the asparagus spears.
2. Divide the asparagus spears into 4 equal bundles, with 4 spears in each bundle.
3. Take a slice of bacon and wrap it tightly around one bundle of asparagus, starting from the bottom and spiralling towards the top. Repeat with the remaining bundles.
4. Preheat the Air Fryer to 200°C for 5 minutes.
5. Lightly brush or spray the Air Fryer basket with olive oil.
6. Place the bacon-wrapped asparagus bundles in the Air Fryer basket, seam side down. Season with salt and black pepper.
7. Air fry at 200°C for 8-10 minutes, flipping halfway through cooking, until the bacon is crispy and the asparagus is tender.
8. Remove the bundles from the Air Fryer and drizzle with balsamic glaze before serving. They make a tasty appetiser or side dish.

Panko Crusted Avocado Fries with Chipotle Lime Ranch

Serves: 4
Prep time: 20 minutes / Cook time: 10 minutes

Ingredients:

- 2 large avocados
- 60g all-purpose flour
- 2 large eggs, beaten
- 120g panko breadcrumbs
- 1/2 tsp paprika
- 1/4 tsp garlic powder
- 1/4 tsp salt
- Vegetable oil, for frying

For the chipotle lime ranch:

- 120ml mayonnaise
- 2 tbsp sour cream
- 1 tbsp lime juice
- 1 tsp chipotle hot sauce
- 1/4 tsp garlic powder
- 1/4 tsp dried dill
- Salt and black pepper, to taste

Preparation instructions:

1. Cut the avocados in half, remove the pits, and cut each half into 4-5 slices.
2. Place the all-purpose flour, beaten eggs, and panko breadcrumbs in separate shallow bowls.
3. In a small bowl, combine the paprika, garlic powder, and salt.
4. Dip each avocado slice into the flour, shaking off any excess. Then dip it into the beaten eggs, allowing any excess to drip off. Finally, coat it in the panko breadcrumbs, pressing lightly to adhere. Repeat with the remaining avocado slices.
5. Preheat the Air Fryer to 200°C for 5 minutes.
6. Lightly brush or spray the Air Fryer basket with vegetable oil.
7. Place the breaded avocado slices in the Air Fryer basket in a single layer, ensuring they are not touching.
8. Air fry at 200°C for 8-10 minutes, flipping halfway through cooking, until the avocado fries are golden brown and crispy.
9. While the avocado fries are cooking, prepare the chipotle lime ranch by combining the mayonnaise, sour cream, lime juice, chipotle hot sauce, garlic powder, dried dill, salt, and black pepper in a small bowl. Mix well.
10. Serve the panko crusted avocado fries with the chipotle lime ranch. They make a delicious appetiser or snack.

Cheesy Spinach and Artichoke Stuffed Mushrooms

Serves: 4
Prep time: 15 minutes / Cook time: 12 minutes

Ingredients:

- 8 large button mushrooms
- 60g cream cheese, softened
- 60g shredded mozzarella cheese
- 30g grated Parmesan cheese
- 60g frozen chopped spinach, thawed and squeezed dry
- 60g canned artichoke hearts, drained and chopped
- 1 clove garlic, minced
- 1 tbsp chopped fresh parsley
- Salt and black pepper, to taste

Preparation instructions:

1. Remove the stems from the mushrooms and set aside. Place the mushroom caps on a plate.
2. In a bowl, combine the cream cheese, shredded mozzarella cheese, grated Parmesan cheese, chopped spinach, chopped artichoke hearts, minced garlic, chopped fresh parsley, salt, and black pepper. Mix well.
3. Spoon the cheese and vegetable mixture into the mushroom caps, filling them generously.
4. Preheat the Air Fryer to 180°C for 5 minutes.
5. Lightly brush or spray the Air Fryer basket with olive oil.
6. Place the stuffed mushrooms in the Air Fryer basket, making sure they are not touching.
7. Air fry at 180°C for 10-12 minutes, until the mushrooms are tender and the cheese is melted and bubbly.
8. Remove from the Air Fryer and let cool for a few minutes before serving. They make a delicious appetiser or side dish.

Jalapeno Popper Stuffed Mini Bell Peppers

Serves: 4
Prep time: 15 minutes / Cook time: 12 minutes

Ingredients:

- 8 mini bell peppers
- 60g cream cheese, softened
- 60g shredded cheddar cheese
- 2 jalapeno peppers, seeded and finely chopped

- 2 green onions, thinly sliced
- 1/4 tsp garlic powder
- 1/4 tsp onion powder
- Salt and black pepper, to taste

Preparation instructions:
1. Slice each mini bell pepper in half lengthwise and remove the seeds and membranes. Place the pepper halves on a plate.
2. In a bowl, combine the cream cheese, shredded cheddar cheese, finely chopped jalapeno peppers, sliced green onions, garlic powder, onion powder, salt, and black pepper. Mix well.
3. Spoon the cheese and jalapeno mixture into the pepper halves, filling them generously.
4. Preheat the Air Fryer to 180°C for 5 minutes.
5. Lightly brush or spray the Air Fryer basket with olive oil.
6. Place the stuffed mini bell peppers in the Air Fryer basket, making sure they are not touching.
7. Air fry at 180°C for 10-12 minutes, until the peppers are tender and the cheese is melted and slightly golden.
8. Remove from the Air Fryer and let cool for a few minutes before serving. They make a delicious appetiser or snack.

Honey Sriracha Glazed Meatballs with Sesame Seeds

Serves: 4
Prep time: 20 minutes / Cook time: 12 minutes

Ingredients:
- 400g ground beef
- 60g breadcrumbs
- 60g finely chopped onion
- 1 clove garlic, minced
- 1 large egg, beaten
- 2 tbsp soy sauce
- 1 tbsp honey
- 1 tbsp sriracha sauce
- 1/2 tsp ground ginger
- 2 tbsp sesame seeds
- 2 green onions, thinly sliced

Preparation instructions:
1. In a bowl, combine the ground beef, breadcrumbs, chopped onion, minced garlic, beaten egg, soy sauce, honey, sriracha sauce, and ground ginger.

Mix well until all the Ingredients are evenly incorporated.
2. Shape the mixture into small meatballs, approximately 2.5cm in diameter.
3. Preheat the Air Fryer to 200°C for 5 minutes.
4. Lightly brush or spray the Air Fryer basket with vegetable oil.
5. Place the meatballs in the Air Fryer basket, making sure they are not touching.
6. Air fry at 200°C for 10-12 minutes, shaking the basket halfway through cooking, until the meatballs are cooked through and browned.
7. In a small bowl, combine the sesame seeds and thinly sliced green onions.
8. Once the meatballs are cooked, remove them from the Air Fryer and roll them in the sesame seed and green onion mixture, ensuring they are coated evenly.
9. Serve the honey sriracha glazed meatballs as an appetiser or as part of a main course. They pair well with rice or noodles.

Spicy Cajun Shrimp Skewers with Remoulade Sauce

Serves: 4
Prep time: 15 minutes / Cook time: 6 minutes

Ingredients:
- 500g large shrimp, peeled and deveined
- 2 tbsp olive oil
- 1 tbsp Cajun seasoning
- 1/2 tsp garlic powder
- 1/2 tsp paprika
- 1/4 tsp cayenne pepper (adjust to taste)
- Salt and black pepper, to taste

For the remoulade sauce:
- 120ml mayonnaise
- 1 tbsp Dijon mustard
- 1 tbsp chopped fresh parsley
- 1 tbsp chopped fresh chives
- 1 clove garlic, minced
- 1 tbsp lemon juice
- 1/4 tsp paprika
- Salt and black pepper, to taste

Preparation instructions:
1. In a bowl, combine the peeled and deveined shrimp, olive oil, Cajun seasoning, garlic powder, paprika, cayenne pepper, salt, and black pepper.

Toss until the shrimp are evenly coated with the seasoning mixture.

2. Preheat the Air Fryer to 200°C for 5 minutes.

3. Lightly brush or spray the Air Fryer basket with olive oil.

4. Thread the seasoned shrimp onto skewers, ensuring they are evenly spaced.

5. Place the shrimp skewers in the Air Fryer basket, making sure they are not touching.

6. Air fry at 200°C for 5-6 minutes, flipping the skewers halfway through cooking, until the shrimp are pink and cooked through.

7. While the shrimp are cooking, prepare the remoulade sauce by combining the mayonnaise, Dijon mustard, chopped fresh parsley, chopped fresh chives, minced garlic, lemon juice, paprika, salt, and black pepper in a small bowl. Mix well.

8. Serve the spicy Cajun shrimp skewers with the remoulade sauce. They make a flavorful appetiser or main course.

Crispy Coconut Onion Rings with Pineapple Dipping Sauce

Serves: 4
Prep time: 20 minutes / Cook time: 10 minutes

Ingredients:

- 2 large onions, cut into 1cm rings
- 60g all-purpose flour
- 2 large eggs, beaten
- 60g shredded coconut
- 1/2 tsp paprika
- 1/4 tsp garlic powder
- 1/4 tsp salt
- Vegetable oil, for frying

For the pineapple dipping sauce:

- 120ml pineapple juice
- 2 tbsp mayonnaise
- 1 tbsp Dijon mustard
- 1 tbsp honey
- 1/4 tsp garlic powder
- Salt and black pepper, to taste

Preparation instructions:

1. Separate the onion rings and set aside.

2. Place the all-purpose flour, beaten eggs, and shredded coconut in separate shallow bowls.

3. In a small bowl, combine the paprika, garlic powder, and salt.

4. Dip each onion ring into the flour, shaking off any excess. Then dip it into the beaten eggs, allowing any excess to drip off. Finally, coat it in the shredded coconut, pressing lightly to adhere. Repeat with the remaining onion rings.

5. Preheat the Air Fryer to 200°C for 5 minutes.

6. Lightly brush or spray the Air Fryer basket with vegetable oil.

7. Place the breaded onion rings in the Air Fryer basket in a single layer, ensuring they are not touching.

8. Air fry at 200°C for 8-10 minutes, flipping halfway through cooking, until the onion rings are golden brown and crispy.

9. While the onion rings are cooking, prepare the pineapple dipping sauce by combining the pineapple juice, mayonnaise, Dijon mustard, honey, garlic powder, salt, and black pepper in a small saucepan. Heat over low heat, stirring constantly, until warmed through.

10. Serve the crispy coconut onion rings with the pineapple dipping sauce. They make a delightful appetiser or snack.

Loaded Mexican Street Corn Dip with Tortilla Chips

Serves: 4
Prep time: 15 minutes / Cook time: 10 minutes

Ingredients:

- 200g canned corn kernels, drained
- 60g mayonnaise
- 60g sour cream
- 60g shredded cheddar cheese
- 2 tbsp finely chopped fresh cilantro
- 1 tbsp lime juice
- 1/2 tsp chilli powder
- 1/4 tsp garlic powder
- 1/4 tsp smoked paprika
- Salt and black pepper, to taste
- Tortilla chips, for serving

Preparation instructions:

1. Preheat the Air Fryer to 180°C for 5 minutes.

2. In a bowl, combine the corn kernels, mayonnaise, sour cream, shredded cheddar cheese, chopped fresh cilantro, lime juice, chilli powder, garlic powder, smoked paprika, salt, and black pepper. Mix well until all the Ingredients are evenly incorporated.

3. Transfer the corn mixture to an oven-safe dish that fits inside the Air Fryer basket.
4. Place the dish in the Air Fryer basket and air fry at 180°C for 8-10 minutes, until the dip is heated through and the cheese is melted and bubbly.
5. Remove from the Air Fryer and let cool for a few minutes before serving.
6. Serve the loaded Mexican street corn dip with tortilla chips for dipping. It's a delicious appetiser or party snack.

Spicy Tandoori Chicken Skewers with Mint Chutney

Serves: 4
Prep time: 20 minutes (+marinating time) / Cook time: 10 minutes

Ingredients:
- 400g boneless, skinless chicken breasts, cut into 2.5cm cubes
- 120g plain yoghurt
- 2 tbsp lemon juice
- 2 tbsp tandoori masala
- 1 tbsp vegetable oil
- 1 clove garlic, minced
- 1/2 tsp ground cumin
- 1/2 tsp ground coriander
- 1/4 tsp cayenne pepper (adjust to taste)
- Salt, to taste

For the mint chutney:
- 60g fresh mint leaves
- 30g fresh cilantro leaves
- 1 green chilli, seeded
- 1 clove garlic
- 2 tbsp lemon juice
- 2 tbsp water
- 1/2 tsp sugar
- Salt, to taste

Preparation instructions:
1. In a bowl, combine the plain yoghurt, lemon juice, tandoori masala, vegetable oil, minced garlic, ground cumin, ground coriander, cayenne pepper, and salt. Mix well to make the marinade.
2. Add the chicken cubes to the marinade and toss to coat them evenly. Cover the bowl and let the chicken marinate in the refrigerator for at least 1 hour, or preferably overnight.
3. Preheat the Air Fryer to 200°C for 5 minutes.

4. Thread the marinated chicken cubes onto skewers, ensuring they are evenly spaced.
5. Place the chicken skewers in the Air Fryer basket, making sure they are not touching.
6. Air fry at 200°C for 8-10 minutes, flipping the skewers halfway through cooking, until the chicken is cooked through and slightly charred.
7. While the chicken is cooking, prepare the mint chutney by combining the fresh mint leaves, fresh cilantro leaves, green chilli, clove of garlic, lemon juice, water, sugar, and salt in a blender or food processor. Blend until smooth.
8. Serve the spicy tandoori chicken skewers with the mint chutney. They make a flavorful appetiser or main course.

Greek Spanakopita Triangles with Tzatziki Sauce

Serves: 4
Prep time: 20 minutes / Cook time: 10 minutes

Ingredients:
- 200g frozen spinach, thawed and drained
- 100g feta cheese, crumbled
- 50g ricotta cheese
- 1 small onion, finely chopped
- 2 cloves garlic, minced
- 2 tbsp chopped fresh dill
- 2 tbsp chopped fresh parsley
- 1/4 tsp dried oregano
- Salt and black pepper, to taste
- 8 sheets filo pastry
- 60 ml melted butter

For the tzatziki sauce:
- 150g Greek yoghurt
- 1/2 cucumber, grated and squeezed to remove excess moisture
- 1 clove garlic, minced
- 1 tbsp lemon juice
- 1 tbsp chopped fresh dill
- Salt and black pepper, to taste

Preparation instructions:
1. Preheat the Air Fryer to 180°C for 5 minutes.
2. In a bowl, combine the thawed and drained spinach, crumbled feta cheese, ricotta cheese, chopped onion, minced garlic, chopped fresh dill, chopped fresh parsley, dried oregano, salt, and black pepper. Mix well to create the filling.

3. Lay one sheet of filo pastry on a clean surface and brush it with melted butter. Place another sheet of filo pastry on top and brush with butter. Repeat this process with two more sheets of filo pastry, brushing each layer with melted butter.

4. Cut the buttered filo pastry stack into 4 equal strips.

5. Spoon a small amount of the spinach and cheese filling onto the bottom corner of each strip. Fold the corner over the filling to form a triangle and continue folding the strip in a triangle shape until the end. Repeat with the remaining filo pastry and filling.

6. Place the spanakopita triangles in the Air Fryer basket in a single layer, making sure they are not touching.

7. Air fry at 180°C for 8-10 minutes, or until the triangles are golden brown and crispy.

8. While the triangles are cooking, prepare the tzatziki sauce by combining the Greek yoghurt, grated cucumber, minced garlic, lemon juice, chopped fresh dill, salt, and black pepper in a bowl. Mix well.

9. Serve the Greek spanakopita triangles with the tzatziki sauce. They make a delicious appetiser or snack.

Smoky Bacon-Wrapped Jalapeno Poppers with Cream Cheese

Serves: 4
Prep time: 15 minutes / Cook time: 10 minutes

Ingredients:
- 8 large jalapeno peppers
- 100g cream cheese
- 50g shredded cheddar cheese
- 1/2 tsp smoked paprika
- 1/4 tsp garlic powder
- 8 slices bacon, halved lengthwise and cut into strips
- Toothpicks, for securing the bacon

Preparation instructions:
1. Preheat the Air Fryer to 200°C for 5 minutes.
2. Cut each jalapeno pepper in half lengthwise and remove the seeds and membranes.
3. In a bowl, mix together the cream cheese, shredded cheddar cheese, smoked paprika, and garlic powder until well combined.
4. Spoon the cream cheese mixture into each

jalapeno half, filling them evenly.

5. Wrap each jalapeno half with a strip of bacon and secure with a toothpick.

6. Place the bacon-wrapped jalapeno poppers in the Air Fryer basket in a single layer, making sure they are not touching.

7. Air fry at 200°C for 8-10 minutes, or until the bacon is crispy and the peppers are tender.

8. Carefully remove the jalapeno poppers from the Air Fryer and let them cool for a few minutes before serving. Remove the toothpicks before eating.

9. These smoky bacon-wrapped jalapeno poppers are perfect as an appetiser or party snack.

Pesto and Sun-Dried Tomato Pinwheels with Balsamic Glaze

Serves: 4
Prep time: 15 minutes / Cook time: 10 minutes

Ingredients:
- 4 sheets puff pastry, thawed
- 4 tbsp basil pesto
- 50g sun-dried tomatoes, chopped
- 50g shredded mozzarella cheese
- 1 egg, beaten
- Balsamic glaze, for drizzling

Preparation instructions:
1. Preheat the Air Fryer to 180°C for 5 minutes.
2. On a lightly floured surface, roll out each sheet of puff pastry into a rectangle.
3. Spread 1 tablespoon of basil pesto evenly over each puff pastry sheet.
4. Sprinkle the chopped sun-dried tomatoes and shredded mozzarella cheese over the pesto.
5. Starting from one of the long sides, tightly roll up the puff pastry sheet into a log.
6. Cut each log into 1.5cm slices to create pinwheels.
7. Place the pinwheels in the Air Fryer basket in a single layer, making sure they are not touching.
8. Brush the pinwheels with beaten egg to give them a golden brown colour.
9. Air fry at 180°C for 8-10 minutes, or until the pinwheels are puffed up and golden brown.
10. Remove the pinwheels from the Air Fryer and let them cool for a few minutes.
11. Drizzle the pesto and sun-dried tomato pinwheels with balsamic glaze before serving. They make a delightful appetiser or finger food.

Teriyaki Glazed Chicken Meatball Skewers with Peanut Sauce

Serves: 4
Prep time: 20 minutes (+chilling time) / Cook time: 10 minutes

Ingredients:
For the chicken meatballs:
- 400g ground chicken
- 60g breadcrumbs
- 60g finely chopped onion
- 2 cloves garlic, minced
- 2 tbsp soy sauce
- 1 tbsp honey
- 1/2 tsp grated fresh ginger
- 1/4 tsp black pepper
- 60g chopped fresh cilantro
- 1 green onion, finely chopped
- 1 tbsp vegetable oil

For the teriyaki glaze:
- 3 tbsp soy sauce
- 2 tbsp honey
- 1 tbsp rice vinegar
- 1 clove garlic, minced
- 1/2 tsp grated fresh ginger

For the peanut sauce:
- 4 tbsp smooth peanut butter
- 2 tbsp soy sauce
- 1 tbsp honey
- 1 tbsp rice vinegar
- 1 clove garlic, minced
- 2-3 tbsp water, as needed

Preparation instructions:
1. In a bowl, combine the ground chicken, breadcrumbs, chopped onion, minced garlic, soy sauce, honey, grated ginger, black pepper, chopped fresh cilantro, and finely chopped green onion. Mix well until all the Ingredients are evenly incorporated.
2. Shape the chicken mixture into small meatballs and place them on a plate. Chill in the refrigerator for at least 30 minutes to firm up.
3. Preheat the Air Fryer to 200°C for 5 minutes.
4. In a small bowl, whisk together the soy sauce, honey, rice vinegar, minced garlic, and grated ginger to make the teriyaki glaze.
5. Brush the meatballs with vegetable oil and place them in the Air Fryer basket in a single layer, making sure they are not touching.
6. Air fry at 200°C for 8-10 minutes, or until the meatballs are cooked through and golden brown.
7. While the meatballs are cooking, prepare the peanut sauce by whisking together the peanut butter, soy sauce, honey, rice vinegar, minced garlic, and enough water to achieve a smooth and pourable consistency.
8. Remove the meatballs from the Air Fryer and brush them with the teriyaki glaze.
9. Thread the meatballs onto skewers and serve with the peanut sauce for dipping. Enjoy these flavorful teriyaki glazed chicken meatball skewers as a delicious appetiser or main dish.

Baked Feta with Honey and Thyme with Toasted Baguette Slices

Serves: 4
Prep time: 10 minutes / Cook time: 15 minutes

Ingredients:
- 200g feta cheese
- 2 tbsp honey
- 1 tsp fresh thyme leaves
- 1 small baguette, sliced
- 2 tbsp olive oil

Preparation instructions:
1. Preheat the Air Fryer to 180°C for 5 minutes.
2. Place the feta cheese in a small oven-safe dish.
3. Drizzle the honey over the feta cheese and sprinkle with fresh thyme leaves.
4. Place the dish with the feta cheese in the Air Fryer basket.
5. Air fry at 180°C for 12-15 minutes, or until the feta cheese is soft and lightly golden.
6. While the feta cheese is cooking, brush the baguette slices with olive oil.
7. Arrange the baguette slices in a single layer in the Air Fryer basket.
8. Air fry at 180°C for 3-5 minutes, or until the baguette slices are toasted and crispy.
9. Remove the baked feta cheese and toasted baguette slices from the Air Fryer.
10. Serve the baked feta cheese warm with the toasted baguette slices. It makes a delicious appetiser or snack.

Buffalo Cauliflower and Chickpea Lettuce Wraps with Ranch Dressing

Serves: 4
Prep time: 15 minutes / Cook time: 15 minutes

Ingredients:
For the buffalo cauliflower and chickpeas:
- 400g cauliflower florets
- 200g canned chickpeas, rinsed and drained
- 2 tbsp hot sauce
- 1 tbsp melted butter
- 1/2 tsp garlic powder
- 1/2 tsp onion powder
- Salt and black pepper, to taste
- 1 tbsp olive oil

For the ranch dressing:
- 150ml Greek yoghurt
- 2 tbsp mayonnaise
- 1 tbsp chopped fresh dill
- 1 tbsp chopped fresh parsley
- 1 clove garlic, minced
- 1 tbsp lemon juice
- Salt and black pepper, to taste

For the lettuce wraps:
- 8 large lettuce leaves
- 1 carrot, grated
- 1 celery stalk, thinly sliced

Preparation instructions:
1. Preheat the Air Fryer to 200°C for 5 minutes.
2. In a bowl, combine the cauliflower florets, chickpeas, hot sauce, melted butter, garlic powder, onion powder, salt, black pepper, and olive oil. Toss well to coat.
3. Place the cauliflower and chickpea mixture in the Air Fryer basket.
4. Air fry at 200°C for 12-15 minutes, or until the cauliflower is tender and lightly charred.
5. While the cauliflower and chickpeas are cooking, prepare the ranch dressing by combining the Greek yoghurt, mayonnaise, chopped dill, chopped parsley, minced garlic, lemon juice, salt, and black pepper in a bowl. Mix well.
6. To assemble the lettuce wraps, place a spoonful of the buffalo cauliflower and chickpea mixture on each lettuce leaf.
7. Top with grated carrot and sliced celery.
8. Drizzle the ranch dressing over the filling.
9. Roll up the lettuce leaves and secure with toothpicks, if needed.
10. Serve the buffalo cauliflower and chickpea lettuce wraps as a flavourful and healthy appetiser or light meal.

Crispy Baked Coconut Shrimp with Mango Salsa

Serves: 4
Prep time: 15 minutes / Cook time: 10 minutes

Ingredients:
For the coconut shrimp:
- 300g large shrimp, peeled and deveined
- 60g all-purpose flour
- 2 eggs, beaten
- 100g shredded coconut
- 1/2 tsp garlic powder
- 1/2 tsp paprika
- Salt and black pepper, to taste

For the mango salsa:
- 1 ripe mango, diced
- 1/2 red bell pepper, diced
- 1/4 red onion, finely chopped
- 1 small jalapeno, seeded and minced
- 2 tbsp chopped fresh cilantro
- 1 tbsp lime juice
- Salt and black pepper, to taste

Preparation instructions:
1. Preheat the Air Fryer to 200°C for 5 minutes.
2. In three separate bowls, place the flour, beaten eggs, and shredded coconut.
3. Season the shrimp with garlic powder, paprika, salt, and black pepper.
4. Dredge each shrimp in flour, dip in beaten eggs, and coat with shredded coconut, pressing gently to adhere.
5. Place the coated shrimp in the Air Fryer basket in a single layer.
6. Air fry at 200°C for 8-10 minutes, or until the shrimp are crispy and golden.
7. While the shrimp are cooking, prepare the mango salsa by combining the diced mango, diced red bell pepper, finely chopped red onion, minced jalapeno, chopped cilantro, lime juice, salt, and black pepper in a bowl. Mix well.
8. Serve the crispy baked coconut shrimp with the mango salsa as a delightful appetiser or party snack.

Crispy Air Fryer Tofu Bites

Serves: 2-4 people
Prep time: 15-20 minutes | Cook time: 15-18 minutes

Ingredients:

- 250g firm tofu, pressed and cut into bite-sized cubes
- 30g cornflour
- 5g garlic powder
- 5g paprika
- 2g salt
- 30 ml soy sauce
- 15 ml maple syrup
- 15 ml sesame oil
- Sesame seeds (for garnish)
- Chopped green onions (for garnish)

Preparation instructions:

1. Preheat the air fryer to 200°C (400°F).
2. In a shallow bowl, combine the cornflour, garlic powder, paprika, and salt. Mix well.
3. In a separate bowl, whisk together the soy sauce, maple syrup, and sesame oil.
4. Dip each tofu cube into the soy sauce mixture, allowing any excess to drip off.
5. Coat the tofu cube in the cornflour mixture, pressing lightly to adhere.
6. Place the coated tofu cubes in the air fryer basket, leaving space between them.
7. Air fry for 15-18 minutes, shaking the basket halfway through, until the tofu is crispy and golden.
8. Remove the tofu bites from the air fryer and let them cool for a few minutes.
9. Sprinkle with sesame seeds and chopped green onions for garnish.
10. Serve the Crispy Air Fryer Tofu Bites as a tasty appetiser or snack, and pair them with your favourite dipping sauce.

Crispy Air Fryer Tortilla Chips

Serves: 2-4 people
Prep time: 10-15 minutes | Cook time: 6-8 minutes

Ingredients:

- 4 large flour tortillas or corn tortillas
- 30 ml olive oil
- 5g chilli powder
- 5g cumin
- 5g garlic powder
- Salt to taste

Preparation instructions:

1. Preheat the air fryer to 180°C (350°F).
2. Stack the tortillas and cut them into wedges, similar to pizza slices.
3. In a bowl, combine the olive oil, chilli powder, cumin, garlic powder, and salt. Mix well.
4. Brush the tortilla wedges with the olive oil mixture, ensuring they are evenly coated.
5. Place the coated tortilla wedges in a single layer in the air fryer basket, leaving space between them.
6. Air fry for 6-8 minutes, flipping the chips halfway through, until they are golden brown and crispy.
7. Remove from the air fryer and let them cool for a few minutes.
8. Serve the crispy air fryer tortilla chips with your favourite salsa, guacamole, or dip.

Cheesy Bacon-Wrapped Jalapeno Poppers with Cream Cheese Filling

Serves: 4
Prep time: 20 minutes / Cook time: 15 minutes

Ingredients:

- 8 jalapeno peppers
- 200g cream cheese, softened
- 100g shredded cheddar cheese
- 1/2 tsp garlic powder
- 8 slices bacon, halved
- Toothpicks, for securing

Preparation instructions:

1. Preheat the Air Fryer to 190°C for 5 minutes.
2. Slice the jalapeno peppers in half lengthwise and remove the seeds and membranes.
3. In a bowl, mix together the softened cream cheese, shredded cheddar cheese, and garlic powder until well combined.
4. Fill each jalapeno half with the cream cheese filling.
5. Wrap each stuffed jalapeno half with a halved slice of bacon and secure with toothpicks.
6. Place the bacon-wrapped jalapeno poppers in the Air Fryer basket.
7. Air fry at 190°C for 12-15 minutes, or until the bacon is crispy and the peppers are tender.
8. Remove the toothpicks before serving.
9. Enjoy the cheesy bacon-wrapped jalapeno poppers as a delicious appetiser or game-day snack.

Printed in Great Britain
by Amazon